Adoption

OTHER BOOKS OF RELATED INTEREST

Adoption

Allen Verbrugge, *Book Editor*

Bruce Glassman, *Vice President*
Bonnie Szumski, *Publisher*
Helen Cothran, *Managing Editor*
David M. Haugen, *Series Editor*

Contemporary Issues
Companion

GREENHAVEN PRESS
An imprint of Thomson Gale, a part of The Thomson Corporation

THOMSON
GALE

Detroit • New York • San Francisco • San Diego • New Haven, Conn.
Waterville, Maine • London • Munich

For more information, contact
Greenhaven Press
27500 Drake Rd.
Farmington Hills, MI 48331-3535
Or you can visit our Internet site at http://www.gale.com

Greenhaven Press anthologies primarily consist of previously published material taken from a variety of sources, including periodicals, books, scholarly journals, newspapers, government documents, and position papers from private and public organizations. These original sources are often edited for length and to ensure their accessibility for a young adult audience. The anthology editors also change the original titles of these works in order to clearly present the main thesis of each viewpoint and to explicitly indicate the opinion presented in the viewpoint. These alterations are made in consideration of both the reading and comprehension levels of a young adult audience. Every effort is made to ensure that Greenhaven Press accurately reflects the original intent of the authors included in this anthology.

LIBRARY OF CONGRESS CATALOGING-IN-PUBLICATION DATA

Adoption / Allen Verbrugge, book editor.
    p. cm. — (Contemporary issues companion)
    Includes bibliographical references and index.
    ISBN 0-7377-2440-4 (lib. : alk. paper) — ISBN 0-7377-2441-2 (pbk. : alk. paper)
    1. Adoption. 2. Adoption—United States. I. Verbrugge, Allen. II. Series.
    HV875.A315 2006
    362.734—dc22   2005050388

Contents

Chapter 5: Personal Stories of Adoption

FOREWORD

In the news, on the streets, and in neighborhoods, individuals are confronted with a variety of social problems. Such problems may affect people directly: A young woman may struggle with depression, suspect a friend of having bulimia, or watch a loved one battle cancer. And even the issues that do not directly affect her private life—such as religious cults, domestic violence, or legalized gambling—still impact the larger society in which she lives. Discovering and analyzing the complexities of issues that encompass communal and societal realms as well as the world of personal experience is a valuable educational goal in the modern world.

Effectively addressing social problems requires familiarity with a constantly changing stream of data. Becoming well informed about today's controversies is an intricate process that often involves reading myriad primary and secondary sources, analyzing political debates, weighing various experts' opinions—even listening to first-hand accounts of those directly affected by the issue. For students and general observers, this can be a daunting task because of the sheer volume of information available in books, periodicals, on the evening news, and on the Internet. Researching the consequences of legalized gambling, for example, might entail sifting through congressional testimony on gambling's societal effects, examining private studies on Indian gaming, perusing numerous websites devoted to Internet betting, and reading essays written by lottery winners as well as interviews with recovering compulsive gamblers. Obtaining valuable information can be time-consuming—since it often requires researchers to pore over numerous documents and commentaries before discovering a source relevant to their particular investigation.

Greenhaven's Contemporary Issues Companion series seeks to assist this process of research by providing readers with useful and pertinent information about today's complex issues. Each volume in this anthology series focuses on a topic of current interest, presenting informative and thought-provoking selections written from a wide variety of viewpoints. The readings selected by the editors include such diverse sources as personal accounts and case studies, pertinent factual and statistical articles, and relevant commentaries and overviews. This diversity of sources and views, found in every Contemporary Issues Companion, offers readers a broad perspective in one convenient volume.

In addition, each title in the Contemporary Issues Companion series is designed especially for young adults. The selections included in every volume are chosen for their accessibility and are expertly edited in consideration of both the reading and comprehension levels of the audience. The structure of the anthologies also enhances accessibility. An introductory essay places each issue in context and provides helpful facts such as historical background or current statistics and legislation that pertain to the topic. The chapters that follow organize the material and focus on specific aspects of the book's topic. Every essay is introduced by a brief summary of its main points and biographical information about the author. These summaries aid in comprehension and can also serve to direct readers to material of immediate interest and need. Finally, a comprehensive index allows readers to efficiently scan and locate content.

The Contemporary Issues Companion series is an ideal launching point for research on a particular topic. Each anthology in the series is composed of readings taken from an extensive gamut of resources, including periodicals, newspapers, books, government documents, the publications of private and public organizations, and Internet websites. In these volumes, readers will find factual support suitable for use in reports, debates, speeches, and research papers. The anthologies also facilitate further research, featuring a book and periodical bibliography and a list of organizations to contact for additional information.

A perfect resource for both students and the general reader, Greenhaven's Contemporary Issues Companion series is sure to be a valued source of current, readable information on social problems that interest young adults. It is the editors' hope that readers will find the Contemporary Issues Companion series useful as a starting point to formulate their own opinions about and answers to the complex issues of the present day.

INTRODUCTION

When a child is born, some of the circumstances surrounding the birth are dutifully recorded on a mandated government document: a birth certificate. The certificate shows the child's name; the date, time, and place of birth; and details such as weight, length, hospital, attending physician, and the names of the child's parents. These certificates are maintained by various state agencies; in most cases, one can visit the appropriate courthouse or department and, for a nominal fee, obtain a copy.

When a child joins a family through adoption, a version of this process is repeated. A new, amended birth certificate is created for the adopted child. The names of his or her adoptive parents will replace the names of the birth parents on the document; if the child's name is different from the one he or she was given at birth, the new name will also appear on the amended birth certificate. The amended birth certificate is formal, valid, and held as the official record from the time the adoption is finalized onward. The adopted child can eventually use this record to obtain a passport, driver's license, or other state document.

The motivation for the amended birth certificate is understandable: The new birth certificate reflects the child's status as a full member of a new family. There is satisfaction to be had in the thought that the child will embrace every aspect of the family that will raise him or her. The amended birth certificate is viewed as a covenant that binds the new family together. And it serves the adopted child so completely that the child is presumed to have no further need for his or her original birth certificate, which is included in a file—along with court records, adoption agency case records, and other information—and sealed by the court. In keeping with the laws of forty-five states, the original birth certificate is not available to the adopted child, even after the child has grown to adulthood. Out of the common and innocuous process of the issuance of birth certificates, it is this last fact that has created a flash point.

The Controversy

The controversy over open access to an original birth certificate stems from the fact that this document will reveal identifying information—that is, the name of the birth mother. While some nonidentifying information is often provided to adopting parents or birth parents during the process of adoption, any data (names or addresses, for example) that could identify the birth mother to the adoptive family—or vice versa—is not disclosed to any party in a traditional (or "closed") adoption.

Whether or not this anonymity serves the best interest of the adopted child is an issue also debated among adoption stakeholders, but once the adoptee reaches the age of majority, the issue is qualitatively different. When adoptees become adults, some argue, to deny them access to state-held documents available to all other adults is an abrogation of rights. Those who advocate for access to records like original birth certificates argue that America's laws single out adult adoptees, so that they alone among adult citizens are not permitted access to their own birth certificates or personal records.

Those who oppose open access to adoption records counter that a birth mother's right to privacy and confidentiality is enough to keep the birth certificate and adoption records under court seal. They hold that to deny birth mothers permanent confidentiality by releasing identifying information is to threaten the institution of adoption itself.

The disagreement over access to original birth certificates and the identifying information they include is one of the most hotly debated issues surrounding traditional adoption. According to Adam Pertman, executive director of the Evan B. Donaldson Adoption Institute, the issue may be the most contentious that the institution of adoption has ever encountered. In his 2000 book *Adoption Nation: How the Adoption Revolution Is Transforming America* Pertman writes, "Obtaining identifying information is the issue that is radicalizing and galvanizing more of the adoption community than any single concern ever has. It is provoking activism of a type and at a level unprecedented in the history of the institution."

Confidentiality

Both proponents and opponents of unsealing adoption records claim that the "history of the institution" supports their side. Those who support permanently sealed adoption records note that confidentiality has been the standard practice since infant adoptions became more widespread in the 1930s. Open records advocates maintain that sealed records laws are a more recent phenomenon; most states did not legally seal records until the 1940s and 1950s. Furthermore, open records proponents claim, the statutes that sealed adoption records were not enacted to protect birth parent privacy but to shield the adoptive family from stigmas that were then attached to adoption or to prevent a birth parent from interfering in the life of an adopted child. The laws were not intended to prevent an adult from accessing records pertaining directly to him or her.

For opponents of open records, birth mother confidentiality is essential. A birth mother may have married or remarried since placing a child for adoption, and she may have chosen not to disclose to family or friends the event from her past. Open records opponents believe the birth mother's decision should not be overridden by anyone else.

Open records supporters respond that confidentiality was never a guarantee. Furthermore, supporters say that resources such as professional detectives, volunteer searchers, and the power of the Internet make it increasingly likely that an adoptee will discover the identity of his or her birth parent even without access to an original birth certificate. They resent the implication that adult adoptees are out to stalk or endanger birth mothers.

To them, the birth mother confidentiality argument fails on another level as well. The amended birth certificates are issued not when the child is relinquished or placed for adoption, but at the time the child is formally adopted. So if a child remains in foster care or group home environment and is never adopted, he or she maintains access to the original birth certificate.

Those who oppose open records also submit that lack of confidentiality will cause abortion rates to increase and the number of adoptions to decrease. They argue that, if records become available at any time, women who face unwanted pregnancies will view abortion as the only confidential option.

Open records supporters counter these assertions with statistics from states and countries that have always permitted adult adoptees to view adoption records. For example, abortion rates in Kansas and Alaska—two states that never sealed adoption records—were lower (as of 1996) than the national rate. Adoption statistics also seem to discredit the arguments of open records opponents. The National Center for Court Statistics reported that the 1992 rate of adoptions per thousand live births was 31.2 nationally, 53.5 in Alaska, and 48.4 in Kansas. Statistics from Great Britain (a country that grants access to adult adoptees) also indicate no connection between open records policy and abortion or adoption rates.

Alternatives to Open Records: Mutual Consent Registries

The National Council for Adoption (NCFA) is a nonprofit advocacy group representing over 150 adoption agencies and two thousand members across the United States. The NCFA has taken the strongest stance against allowing unconditional access to adoption records. One of the NCFA's policy priorities speaks to the importance of the option of privacy in adoption: "Adoption policy and practice should not empower one party to adoption to receive identifying information or unilaterally impose contacts without the consent of another party. NCFA therefore opposes laws that provide to adult adopted persons, without birthparents' knowledge and consent, unqualified access to original birth certificates or other documentation that identifies the birthparents."

The NCFA stresses that it is not opposed to the disclosure of identifying information, but that such disclosure must be agreed to by the affected parties. Therefore, according to the NCFA, mutual consent registries are the best solution. Mutual consent registries allow adoptees and birth parents to register with a government agency in the state where the adoptee was born or adopted. Names and other identifying information can be released if the parties consent to the release of the information. These registries can either be passive registries (in which parties to an adoption must register independently of one another) or active registries (in which one party registers with an agency, and a third party contacts the person being sought for their consent to have information released). Some form of mutual consent registry is in place in nearly every state, yet such registries are not the equivalent of having unobstructed access to birth records.

To those who support open access to adoption records—groups that include the Child Welfare League of America, Concerned United Birthparents, American Adoption Congress, and the Adoptees' Liberty Movement Association—mutual consent registries are a flawed and woefully inadequate solution. The state-by-state nature of the registries is problematic for adoptees who do not know the location of their birth, or for those born in one state and adopted in another. A lack of funds for staff and publicity make the registries particularly ineffectual in some states. Some registries require permission from adoptive parents before identifying information is distributed, which adult adoptees find condescending and insulting. The most obvious drawback of the registries becomes clear in cases when an adoptee or birth parent is deceased.

Open records supporters also argue against provisions in registries known as disclosure vetoes (filed by one party to register a refusal to the release of identifying information) or contact vetoes (filed to register a refusal to be contacted by the searching party). Open records advocates interpret these provisions as "permissions" that are not necessary for nonadopted adults to obtain, and thus an unfair requirement. Furthermore, advocates argue, mutual consent registries miss the principle of the argument: Adult adoptees should be afforded the same rights as any adult. No other adult would need to negotiate so much bureaucracy in order to view his or her birth certificate.

Progress for Open Records Supporters?

Ultimately, the decisions governing access to original birth certificates and adoption records are left to the states. Under the laws of most states, access to records can only be obtained with a court order. Only five states—Alabama, Alaska, Kansas, New Hampshire, and Oregon—allow adult adoptees unconditional access to their original birth certificates. Many states strive for some sort of middle ground, utilizing mutual consent registries, contact or disclosure vetoes, or granting access to adult adoptees with written consent of the birth parent.

Since 1995 some state legislatures moved to allow access to previously sealed original birth certificates, due in part to activism of open records supporters. In November 1998 Oregon voters approved a ballot initiative to provide adult adoptees unconditional access to their original birth certificates. The law survived legal challenges from opponents of open records and took effect in May 2000. That same month and year, Alabama granted unrestricted access to original birth certificates and adoption records for adult adoptees in that state. The support needed to pass these laws came from national adoptees' rights organizations like Bastard Nation and local groups like Alabamians Working for Adoption Reform and Education (AWARE).

There is no shortage of passion on the side of open records supporters, and the legislative battles in Oregon and Alabama are evidence that their strident advocacy may be paying dividends. Bastard Nation is one of the most outspoken activist groups fighting for open records, and the group articulates its positions with representative fervor. The organization's Web site attests: "We are angry at those self-interested sections of the adoption industry which continue to lobby for sealed records, hiding their own past misdeeds under a cloak of 'birth parent privacy,' and implying that adoptees are potential stalkers who would harm their birth parents if they had access to their own records," the group states. "We are angry that the media still portrays us far too often as 'adopted children,' refusing to let us grow up and take our places as full citizens of this country."

If the tide is turning in favor of access to original birth certificates and other adoption records, activism and fiery rhetoric may earn some of the credit. But level-headed common sense and a basic idea of fairness may play roles as well. Rochelle Harris is the head of an adult adoptee group in Kansas, a state that has always allowed adult adoptees to access adoption records. In a 1998 article for the *Oregonian*, Harris says of the Kansas records, "It's not because we're such a forward state; it's because we just never closed them. There aren't any big lawsuits going on. People aren't throwing themselves off bridges. You just have to stay calm about things. People just get worried about the unknown."

CHAPTER 1

THE ADOPTION PROCESS

Contemporary Issues
Companion

AMERICANS HAVE A FAVORABLE OPINION OF ADOPTION

Dave Thomas Foundation for Adoption and
Evan B. Donaldson Adoption Institute

The Dave Thomas Foundation for Adoption is a nonprofit public charity dedicated to promoting the adoption of children in North America's foster care system. In June 2002 the foundation published the results of a national survey on attitudes toward adoption, conducted by Harris Interactive, a market research firm best known for the Harris Poll. The study asked Americans about topics such as whether they had ever considered adoption; what factors might motivate them to adopt or what concerns might keep them from adopting; and what their perceptions were of adoptive parents, adopted persons, foster care, and other related matters. Attitudes about special needs, international, transracial, and open adoptions were also considered. The results were broken down to factor in differences among genders, races/ethnicities, ages, incomes, and education levels. The following selection is taken from the executive summary of the survey and presents a snapshot of the research findings. The survey was conducted in cooperation with the Evan B. Donaldson Adoption Institute, another national nonprofit organization devoted to improving adoption policy and practice.

In America today, more than 134,000 children wait in foster care for adoptive homes. That is more than enough children to fill any stadium in the country. It's a mid-sized town of children. These children have many characteristics—most are older than five, some have brothers and sisters who need to be adopted together and some have physical or behavioral challenges. . . .

The Dave Thomas Foundation for Adoption and the Evan B. Donaldson Adoption Institute initiated this research to better understand what Americans think about adoption and, in particular, what might influence them to or deter them from adopting children in need of families. . . .

Strong Support for Adoption

Nearly four in ten Americans (39%), or about 81.5 million adults, have considered adopting at some time in their lives. This is up from 36% uncovered in 1997. With 134,000 children in foster care waiting for permanent families, these children would all have a home today if less than 1% of adults who have considered adoption pursued adopting these children. Unfortunately, tens of thousands of boys and girls still languish in foster care because not enough adults who consider adopting actually do it.

The National Adoption Attitudes Survey found that two-thirds of Americans have a favorable opinion about adoption, and two-thirds have a personal experience with adoption. Favorable opinions about adoption are prevalent among all social groups in the United States. Even among groups with the least favorable opinions overall—the very young (18–24), those 65 or older, African-Americans and the least educated—a majority have very favorable opinions about adoption.

Positive opinion of and familiarity with adoption have grown significantly in the last five years. In 1997, 56% of Americans had a very favorable opinion about adoption—today, 63% do. Similarly, 58% had experienced adoption within their family or among close friends in 1997, compared to 64% now.

Other indicators of strong support for adoption include:

- 78% of Americans think the country should be doing more to encourage adoption.
- 95% think that adoptive parents should receive the same maternity and paternity benefits from employers as biological parents.
- Three-fourths (75%) of Americans believe adoptive parents are very likely to love their adoptive children as much as children born to them.
- Over 80% think that parents get as much or more satisfaction from raising adoptive children as from raising biological children.
- Americans also have very positive opinions about adoptive parents. They are seen as lucky by 94% of Americans.

Health, Behavior, and Race

This research explored Americans' willingness to consider adopting children with several different characteristics prevalent among the 134,000 children in the United States foster care system who are available for adoption. These characteristics include different ages, races, mental or physical health problems, and length of time they've been in foster care. When Americans consider adoption, the characteristics of available children prove to be a key factor in their decision.

One of the critical findings is that most Americans reported that they were willing to consider adopting older children and/or children from foster care who were older and/or of a different race. Children with physical and/or behavioral issues raised the most concerns for Americans in considering adoption.

In fact, over three-fourths of Americans say they would be very (40%) or somewhat (37%) likely to consider adopting a child who is of a different race. Similarly, when asked about their concerns when adopting children out of foster care, only 18% said that race was a major concern and only 27% indicated that age was a major concern. Respondents had similar views when specifically asked about adopting older children or children of a race different from them. The survey revealed, however, that Americans had major concerns about the physical and mental health status of children available for adoption in general and from the foster care system in particular, regardless of the age or race of the child.

- Fewer than half of Americans would be very likely (11%) or somewhat likely (36%) to consider adopting a child with behavioral problems.
- Slightly more than half of Americans would be very likely to consider (14%) or somewhat likely to consider (42%) adopting a child with medical problems.
- Nearly two-thirds of Americans (63%) say that the mental health of the child would be a major concern when adopting out of foster care, and over half (53%) reported that the physical health of the child would be a major concern.
- African-Americans and Hispanics are more willing than Whites to consider adopting children with characteristics that may concern prospective parents. This is true across a wide range of situations including adopting a child out of foster care, a child of a different race, or a child with medical or behavioral problems.

Demographic Factors

As stated earlier, 39% of all Americans have "very" or "somewhat" seriously considered adopting a child at some time in their lives. The following shows some demographic details:

- The single most compelling demographic difference is that Hispanic populations have a far greater likelihood to consider adopting (54%) than African-American (45%) and White (36%) populations. Those indicating they have "very seriously considered" adopting are—Hispanic (32%), African-American (23%), White (16%).
- Age is also of a factor in considering adoption. The highest percentage of individuals who have considered adopting are those aged 35–44 (48%) and 45–54 (45%). Those least likely to have considered adopting are those aged 65 and older (21%) and 55–64 (34%).
- Married couples are more likely to have considered adopting (43%) than singles (35%) and the previously married individuals (34%).

- Females are more likely to have considered adopting than males, 42% to 35%, respectively.
- There are no significant differences between different income ranges—thus income is not an indicator on whether someone considers adopting.
- Education is also not a determinant, as those with a high school diploma have the same propensity to consider adopting as those with a college degree. However, those with a graduate degree are slightly more likely to consider adopting (46%).

Adoption from Foster Care

Despite overwhelmingly positive views about adoption and generally positive views of the foster care system, Americans are concerned about the outcomes for adopted children. Forty-one percent of Americans think adopted children in general and almost two-thirds (62%) think children adopted out of foster care are more likely than others to have problems at school. A similar proportion—45% and 68%—think adopted children in general and adopted foster children in particular—are more likely to have behavioral problems. A third (32%) believe adopted children in general and more than half (53%) believe children adopted out of foster care are less likely to be well-adjusted.

The concerns that Americans have about adopting children out of foster care are reflected in the services that they say are most important to them in deciding whether to adopt a child from foster care:

- Over three-fourths (77%) wanted health insurance for pre-existing conditions.
- Over two-thirds (69%) say access to a variety of educational and informational materials would be critical.
- More than half (57%) ask for support groups for the child.
- Half say counseling services for the adoptive parent (50%) and support groups for parents (49%) are needed.

The perceived importance of receiving these support services does not vary based on the age and race of the child.

Some Adoption Concerns

Americans have other concerns about adoption that must be addressed in order to increase the numbers who will consider adopting children. The survey found that four out of five Americans (82%) would be concerned that the birth parents might take the child back, though such instances are extremely rare after a finalized adoption. Also, despite a $10,000 federal adoption tax credit, low to no-cost foster care adoptions and subsidies for adopted foster care children, one in two (50%) Americans say that the cost of adoption is a major concern. Cost concerns almost half of middle income Americans (45%) (those earning from $25,000 to $99,000) who comprise the majority of American households, as well as over half (52%) of lower income Americans.

Other significant concerns that Americans have about adoption include having the time to raise a child (a major concern for 49%) and dealing with unexpected genetic or medical problems that emerge after adoption (a major concern for 44%).

With regard to adoption out of foster care, concerns that were mentioned by at least a third of those surveyed, in addition to the mental and physical health of the child, include:

- Having the financial resources needed to raise the child (a major concern for 49%). It is interesting to note, however, that only 35% say financial assistance would be a very important service to them when thinking about whether to adopt a child out of foster care.
- Having the parenting skills needed to raise the child (a major concern for 45%).
- The amount of time the child has been in foster care (a major concern for 37%).

The survey documents a key perceived difference in why people adopt children of different ages. Nearly two-thirds (63%) of Americans think adults adopt young children primarily to create a family for themselves, and only 20% think most adults adopt young children to provide a good home for children who need one. In other words, the decision to adopt young children is perceived to be driven by the needs of the adults.

The results are just the reverse when Americans think about why people adopt children out of foster care: the same proportion (64%) think it is mainly to provide a good home for children and only 25% think it is to create a family for themselves. The perceptions are the same for the adoption of older children: 67% think parents adopt to provide a good home and 22% think parents adopt to create a family. In short, when asked to consider adopting older and foster children who are currently available for adoption in large numbers, Americans believe that the decision is primarily altruistic and not based on the adults' needs.

Open, International, and Interracial Adoptions

Over the last decade, adoption has undergone significant change. One significant change is the growth of "open adoption," where birth parents, adoptive parents and adopted children have ongoing contact from the beginning of the adoption. Among individuals adopted when contact with birth families was not sanctioned, there are increasing numbers of reports about adopted people seeking out and finding their birth families. Most Americans think it is usually a good thing for the adopted child (68%) and for the adoptive parents (60%) when the child seeks out his or her birth parents. A plurality (49%) also think it is a good idea for the birth parents.

Americans are more divided about "open-adoption." A fifth (21%)

think it is a good idea in most cases, about half (47%) think it is a good idea in some cases, a fifth (21%) think it is a good idea in only a very few cases, and 10% think it is never a good idea. Americans who think that open adoption is a good idea in at least a few cases recognize the benefits it provides to the participants in adoption. Two-thirds (67%) think it is a good idea because it helps children know about their family background; 60% think it is a good idea because it helps the child and their adoptive parents get needed health information; and 73% think it helps the child know that their birth parents care about them.

The survey also sought to understand some of the factors that might have contributed to a three-fold increase in the number of international adoptions in the past decade. Americans think that international adoptions are easier to complete than domestic adoptions by a 50% to 38% margin, with the balance unsure. However, by a 47% to 40% plurality, with the balance undecided, Americans think that a child who is internationally adopted is more likely than a domestically adopted child to have significant medical or emotional problems.

Finally, changes to federal law in the 1990's require states to remove barriers to adoption of foster children by willing families, even families of a different race or ethnic background than the children. The survey explored Americans' perceptions about social barriers to inter-racial adoption involving African-Americans and Whites, finding that more people perceive more disapproval than approval of inter-racial adoption. This is true whether the child is African-American or White and whether the adoptive parents are African-American or White. An interesting finding is that Whites perceive higher levels of disapproval of inter-racial adoption in the African-American community than African-Americans do. African-Americans, however, tend to perceive the same level of disapproval among Whites as Whites themselves do.

When Americans are asked where they would go for information or advice about adopting, more than half would turn to foster care agencies and to social welfare agencies in their communities. Almost half (48%) say they would go to their place of worship and four out of ten would go to friends and neighbors. The Internet would be a source for 29%, primarily younger Americans, and 17% would turn to newspapers, magazines or television.

When asked about their major sources of information about adoption today (as opposed to where they would turn for information if they were thinking about adopting), most Americans say their main sources of information are families and friends and the news media.

Americans tend to view the media as mirroring their own positive perspectives of adoption. They believe that media coverage of adoption is either very (19%) or somewhat (53%) favorable. Only a fifth think that coverage is somewhat (15%) or very (6%) unfavorable, with the balance unsure.

AMERICANS STILL HAVE LINGERING FEARS ABOUT ADOPTION

Kelly King Alexander

In the following article, Kelly King Alexander explores how the adoption process has been transformed in the last few decades. As Alexander notes, the Internet has emerged both as a resource for prospective parents to research the adoption process and as a tool for adoption agencies and foster care organizations to help place children waiting for adoption. Alexander goes on to mention that now the sometimes considerable costs of adoption are being offset by federal tax relief for adoptive parents, agencies that charge fees on a sliding scale, and greater numbers of employers offering adoption benefits and cost reimbursements. Despite such assistance, Alexander notes that Americans still have concerns about the complexity of the adoption process, the cost entailed, and the potential difficulties of dealing with identity issues in adopted children. These fears, Alexander explains, have kept the number of annual adoptions in recent years lower than in previous decades. Kelly King Alexander is a regular contributor to *Parents* magazine, from which this article is taken.

Bradley Bordelon is only 7, but he understands that there are two ways to have children. One is to come out of Mommy's tummy, like he did, and the other is to come on an airplane from Russia, as his 4-year-old-sister, Nadia, did. The lesson was reinforced last May, when Bradley's parents, Karen, 33, and Chad, 32, of Mandeville, Louisiana, returned to Russia to adopt two more children, Benjamin, 3, and Katya, 2—and again this January, when Karen gave birth to his baby sister, Hannah. "Bradley says when he gets married, his wife will have a baby, then they'll adopt." Karen says. "That's normal to him."

Today many adults are discovering a truth that the Bordelon children already know—that there is more than one way to create a family. After decades of secrecy, adoption has come out of the closet. Celebrities regularly speak out about being adoptive parents, and even in the notoriously divided Congress, adoption has become a surprising unifier, attracting 153 members from across the political spectrum to a caucus dedicated to making adoption easier, safer and more affordable.

Interest Increases, Numbers Decrease

The urge to adopt is not limited to couples with fertility problems. More and more couples with biological children are turning to adoption as a way to expand their family, and adoptions by single people, same-sex couples, and "empty nesters" looking to start a second family are also on the rise. In addition, foster-care reform has moved a record number of older children into permanent, adoptive homes.

Ironically, adoption has gained visibility at the same time that the total number of adoptions has decreased. Experts estimate that about 120,000 children are adopted annually in the United States—31 percent fewer than in 1970, a peak year that saw 175,000 adoptions.

Several factors explain the downward trend. Increases access to contraception and abortion—and society's acceptance of what used to be called "unwed" mothers—have made fewer babies available: Between 1989 and 1995, only 1.7 percent of never-married white women relinquished babies for adoption, dropping from 19 percent in the period before 1972, according to the National Center for Health Statistics [NCHS], in Hyattsville, Maryland. The rate among blacks has historically been less than 2 percent for births to unmarried women and now hovers near zero.

Meanwhile, the number of people wanting to adopt has increased— a fact that explains the issue's high profile. A 1997 NCHS survey found that for every domestic adoption, there are five or six would-be parents—nearly double the number a decade earlier.

Yet even as the number of white American infants available for adoption has shrunk, more children of all races and ages, in the U.S. and abroad, are seeking homes. And this paradox has given rise to another: Though the dizzying array of possibilities undeniably gives prospective parents more choice, more voice, and more power, it can also make the adoption process more daunting. But the course can be smoothed by clarifying some common misconceptions and concerns.

Complex Process

Would-be adoptive parents have good reason to feel intimidated: Adoption law varies wildly from state to state, with differences on nearly every issue, from how long after delivery a birth mother can sign relinquishment papers, to the rights of birth fathers and whether birth records are open or sealed. But help may be on the way. "We're trying to create some minimum standards for states," says Cindy

Freidmutter, executive director of the Evan B. Donaldson Adoption Institute, in New York City.

Technology has also transformed adoption. Cases like the infamous "Internet twins"—in which a "facilitator" and a birth mother used the Internet to place twin girls with two different couples—have cast a shadow on the medium, but it can also be an invaluable tool. When Jeanene Cockrell, of Mobile, Alabama, had trouble getting pregnant, she was able to research adoption online, comparing state laws and looking up agencies—all in the comfort of her home. From her research, Cockrell, 40, decided she was most comfortable with adoption laws in Texas, which she feels are clearly defined and have safeguards for all members of the adoption "triad": birth mothers, adoptees, and adoptive parents. She and her husband later adopted Emily Allison, 3, in that state.

U.S. Senator Mary Landrieu, a Louisiana Democrat who cochairs the congressional coalition, also touts the virtues of the Internet. An adoptive mother herself, Landrieu supports funding for a government Website that disseminates adoption information (www.calib.com/ naic), as well as a Website for the National Adoption Center, which posts photographs of children waiting to be adopted from foster care (www.adopt.org). "The Internet is the best friend these kids have ever had," Landrieu insists.

Lisa Hofmann, a community producer of Adoption Central, Parent Soup's online-adoption community, found her 4-year-old son on the Precious In His Sight photo listing (www.precious.org). Because he was in foster care in South Korea, it's unlikely she would have found him otherwise.

The average time it takes to adopt a healthy infant in the U.S. varies widely, from about a year to seven years. The wait is shorter for international adoptions—from six to 24 months. And the adoption of a child from foster care can be even quicker.

Adoption Costs

Adoption *can* be costly. According to the National Endowment for Financial Education, in Englewood, Colorado, adoptions of healthy infants in the U.S. and children from abroad typically cost $5,000 to $25,000.

But not all adoptions cost so much. "Waiting children" (the term for kids in foster care who are available for adoption) and "special needs" children (kids in foster care with physical, developmental, or emotional disabilities) can be adopted from public social-service agencies virtually cost-free and sometimes with subsidies for future care.

There's also federal tax relief in store. The Hope for Children Act of 2001, which was signed into law as part of [a] federal tax-cut package, extends and increases the adoption tax credit to $10,000 for adoptive couples who earn less than $150,000.

About a third of U.S. employers also offer adoption benefits. The most common is reimbursing employees for a portion of their fees. For example, Gruner + Jahr USA, the corporation that owns *Parents*, pays up to $4,000 toward the cost of each adoption.

Federal tax relief and employer benefits, however, come after the fact. "You still have to spend the money up front," notes Norman Hecht Jr., an adoptive father and a banker in Rockville, Maryland, who introduced the concept of "adoption loans" to banking ten years ago. Hecht advises prospective adoptive parents to look for agencies that offer sliding-scale fees based on income. New York's Spence-Chapin Agency, for example, provides services for $3,000 to someone earning less than $45,000. "We really try to make adoption affordable," says Sandy Ripberger, communications director for Spence-Chapin.

When Matthew and Patricia Blake, 35 and 38, were diagnosed with infertility three years ago, they initially thought they would adopt outside the U.S. But when the St. George, Utah, couple—a massage therapist and a teacher's aide—looked into the cost, they found they couldn't afford the $15,000 in agency fees, which excluded travel. Then they contacted an adoption agency that works through their Mormon church: its sliding-scale fees allowed the Blakes to adopt a baby girl for just under $5,000.

Acquaintances pale when told of the $60,000 Karen and Chad Bordelon have spent to adopt their three children internationally, but Chad, an engineer, compares the monthly note they pay on adoption loans with extra expenses other families don't think twice about. "Instead of buying new cars or remodeling the house," he says, "we're investing in the life of a child."

Contact with Birth Parents

"My worst nightmare was that I'd get a baby and then someone would take her away," Jeanene Cockrell says. This possibility continues to haunt prospective adoptive parents, despite the fact that less than one percent of finalized adoptions are challenged legally, according to the North American Council on Adoptable Children, in Saint Paul. (Experts acknowledge, however, that in up to 30 percent of cases, birth mothers legally change their mind before relinquishment is final.)

That said, the role birth parents play in adoption has unquestionably increased. Often, they screen applicants and choose a couple to be their child's parents. Some states now offer more assistance to birth parents in the form of mandatory preadoption counseling and minimum waiting periods before relinquishment. These safeguards can be scary for adoptive parents, but they actually reduce the risk of a contested adoption. Indeed, experts say, the best way to minimize future legal challenges is to make sure that the rights of the birth mother have been surrendered legally and voluntarily.

Despite the increasing prevalence of open adoptions—in seven of ten adoptions, all parties have met one another—most adoptive parents are afraid of ongoing contact with birth parents. They needn't be. "It's fear of the unknown," says Ron Weltzheimer, of Edmond, Oklahoma, an adoptive father of three: fear that the birth mother will change her mind if she remains in contact, fear that the child won't attach to them if the birth parents are involved, and fear that a third party will intrude in the family's life.

Weltzheimer, who sends letters and photos to his children's birth mothers, originally wanted closed adoptions. He changed his mind after he watched his first child's birth mother hand over the baby. "It was very emotional," he recalls. "She wants the best for the child and likes getting this information."

Issues of Health, Behavioral Problems

Prospective parents also worry about health and behavioral problems because it's often difficult to know whether a child received proper prenatal care or was exposed to drugs and alcohol before birth. Although experts say such problems are rare, they suggest using a reputable agency and gathering as much medical information about the child as possible. In 1994, Christine Wynne, 50, of Oakland, California, was sent a 5-minute video and a brief medical chart on 20-month-old Roman; she brought both to a pediatrician for review. She learned that the Russian-born toddler was underweight, developmentally delayed, and had juvenile cataracts but otherwise appeared healthy. Today, at age 8, Roman Wynne excels academically, musically, and socially.

Karen Bordelon, who adopted three children from Russia, acknowledges that some orphanages have deplorable conditions but argues that most, in her experience, are clean, well kept (if bare), and run by caring staff. "People are so afraid these kids will be damaged," she says. "Then again, I know parents whose biological children have problems. Let's face it—there are no guarantees with any child."

Special Type of Parent

There is no denying that adoption seekers must go through a screening process that no biological parent is ever asked to endure. This contributes to the impression that they are held to a higher standard than other parents are—and in some sense, that's true. Christine Wynne, for example, labored for months over a "Dear Birth Mother" letter as part of her domestic application package. "My lawyer told me, 'This could decide whether you're chosen'," she says. "I agonized over every word."

Though biological parents are no strangers to the pressure to be perfect, the impulse can be acute among those who adopt. One California mother recalls a visit by a social worker a month after she brought her baby home. "I was a wreck. Should he be dressed up or down? Should the house look immaculate or lived in?" she says. "Finally, the social worker told me to relax and enjoy my son."

In fact, adoptive parents need not be rich, married, middle-class, childless, or home owners. They must be financially stable, but more important to placement professionals is a strong desire to love and nurture a child.

As for the fear that adoptive children will have to deal with difficult questions of identity: "Deep down, you're always concerned," acknowledges Weltzheimer. "Is he someday going to say, 'You're not my daddy'?"

"Adopted children do contend with loss and grief at early ages," concedes Joyce Maguire Pavao, author of *The Family of Adoption* (Beacon Press, 1998) and director of the Center for Family Connections, in Cambridge, Massachusetts. "But these issues are not pathological, just different."

Sonya Merrill, of Norwalk, Connecticut, knew about the troubled pasts of her three children when she adopted them from foster care in 1996. Though all are now in good health, two of her daughters (who were born drug-addicted) continue to work through behavioral problems. Like Pavao, Merrill, who already had a biological daughter, feels that these struggles are not unlike those encountered by all children. "People need to stop dwelling on these kids' faults and baggage and start looking at their human need to be loved," she says. "I've got problems, too, and my kids put up with them. What's the big deal?"

Real Families

Americans are ambivalent about adoption: Though 90 percent view it favorably according to a survey by the Donaldson Institute, roughly half believe that adoption is not quite as good as raising a biological child.

Adam Pertman, the author of *Adoption Nation: How the Adoption Revolution Is Transforming America* (Basic Books, 2000), and his wife, Judy, adopted their son and daughter after discovering they were infertile. "Yes, adoption was our second choice, but in no way is it second best," Pertman says. "To love my kids any more, I'd have to grow another heart."

His sentiments are echoed by Matthew Blake, who often draws stares when he is out with his biracial daughters. "A baby doesn't have to have the same skin color or facial features to be yours," says Blake, who has begun advocating publicly for transracial adoption. (His efforts have borne fruit right in his own backyard: When the Blakes brought 2-day-old daughter Phoebe home to their all-white community, she integrated it overnight. Since then, several other families in the Utah town of 50,000 have adopted biracial children.)

As the mother of both biological and adopted children, Karen Bordelon quickly dispels the myth that the emotional bond is different with either. "You don't even remember that you didn't give birth to these kids," she says, her voice choked with emotion.

Senator Landrieu's favorite adoption anecdote also underscores that bottom-line reality. Landrieu had just told a new acquaintance that her children Connor, 8, and Mary Shannon, 3, had been adopted. "What a coincidence!" the elderly gentleman exclaimed. "Two of my four children are also adopted. I just can't remember which two."

Common Decisions That Parents Will Make in the Adoption Process

Richard Mintzer

The following selection is an excerpt from Richard Mintzer's book, Yes, You Can Adopt! The selection is directed toward potential adoptive parents and presents three key decisions made in any adoption: whether to adopt internationally or domestically, whether to adopt a newborn or an older child, and whether the adoption should be "open" or "closed" in regard to future contact with birth parents. Using the situations and comments of adoptive parents, Mintzer shows that these decisions are interrelated, and each decision carries its own benefits and risks. Mintzer is a journalist and author. He has also served as copresident of the New York City chapter of the Adoptive Parents Committee.

You have many choices to make in the adoption process and key decisions that can determine how smoothly you will proceed along the road to adopting your child(ren) and what your forever family will look like. These decisions will overlap greatly. For example, if you decide you want only a newborn baby, you are making two decisions at once. First, you are deciding that you do not want to adopt an older child in the world of adoption, older can mean a few months old; and second, you are making the decision to adopt domestically, since it is nearly impossible to adopt a newborn baby from abroad. Conversely, you will open up several options should you decide that you would be comfortable adopting a child that is eight or nine months of age. In this case international adoption would become possibile. Of course, that opens up yet another question: Will you be comfortable adopting a child of a different ethnic heritage and possibly of a different race? Lots of questions, lots of decisions . . . but you need not make them all at once.

"We attended an adoption conference," says Laurie, who with her husband Fred, are now parents of two children, one adopted domestically and one from overseas. "It was overwhelming at first. Agencies were asking us if we wanted to adopt a child from Eastern Europe, social workers were talking about children from the foster-care system, and one workshop we attended discussed finding a birth mother domestically and adopting a baby here in the United States. We had no idea what manner was the best for us. We knew we wanted a baby in our life, but we weren't ready to make these major decisions." Laurie and Frank took a long weekend at a resort to sort out their many adoption decisions in a relaxing atmosphere.

"A few days away can give you a better perspective," she explains. "We were able to openly discuss how we envisioned our family. We knew we wanted to adopt soon, but the quickest method did not necessarily mean we'd form a family in a manner that would be comfortable for us. I think people need to picture their family and then make decisions that will help them make that picture a reality. People shouldn't adopt in one manner or another because it's cheaper or faster. They should adopt the way they think they can form the family they really desire."

Domestic or International Adoption

One of the first decisions you will make is the part of the world in which you will direct your efforts. The two options you are immediately faced with are whether to adopt domestically or internationally. . . .

We all have preconceptions—and some misconceptions—about the makeup of our future families. While it is easier to imagine the physical appearance and personalities of biological children, adopted children come in many forms. They may not be infants; they may be of a different race or ethnicity. The fact that your family was formed by adoption may or may not be obvious to the world around you depending on which method of adoption you choose. . . .

Amy C., a single mom of a beautiful little girl, recounts a series of conversations with two close friends who were trying to persuade her to go to China to adopt. "Being single, I knew that it would be a little more difficult to adopt. China was certainly a good option for single woman at that time . . . but my heart was set on trying to adopt a newborn baby. The girls being adopted from China were generally around ten months old, and while they were beautiful children, I had always envisioned myself with a newborn baby. I had always thought of myself as married, too, but since that had not yet happened, I felt I should be more prudent about going after what I felt was right for me in my heart. I believed that there would be a newborn baby that was destined to be with me."

Two of Amy's closest friends thought they were being helpful by continually trying to sway her toward adopting from China. "I knew that it was a viable method and that I could go that route, but I just wanted to follow my own heart. It put a lot of pressure on these friendships and I finally had to sit them down one evening and explain that while I appreciated their good intentions, they had to recognize what my wishes were, even if it meant the process would be more difficult. I couldn't even articulate exactly why this meant so much to me, but it did. From that point on they understood and were supportive."

A year and a half later, Amy adopted a newborn baby, born in Indiana.

Conversely, Sheila wanted nothing more than to have a child in her life, and sooner than later. "I knew being a single mom that adopting would be hard, and I just wanted a child very much. I knew there were many little girls in orphanages in China in need of homes, and I wanted to give one a better life." Sheila adopted her daughter after some eight months in the adoption process. She then joined a New York–based organization of families that had adopted children from China to help her learn about the culture and to provide her daughter with information about her heritage. "Everyone around me was very supportive of my decision," she adds. "That was important because it made me feel more confident in what I was doing. I had no problem with adopting from overseas. I couldn't love her more than I do," says Sheila, who brought her daughter LuAnn home when she was fifteen months old. "My parents were worried about whether they would bond with a granddaughter born so far away, but as soon as they saw her, they fell in love with her. Now they spoil her.". . .

Cost and Health Issues

Other significant areas of concern include cost, health issues, and contact with birth parents.

The costs will vary, with international often being less expensive as there are more set fees (i.e., agency fees, orphanage payment, etc.) and fewer variables. However, the travel, including one or more trips to the country, can add up. These costs will often make international and domestic adoption rather comparable from a financial standpoint. Both methods of adoption will generally fall in the $15,000 to $25,000 range unless there are complications (e.g., additional lawyer fees), which can raise the total expenditure.

Medical issues are generally a greater concern when adopting internationally. While some countries, like Colombia, provide detailed health information, many other countries do not have the same information readily available. It is, however, important to note that despite the added concern because of the limited data available, the vast majority of children adopted internationally have few significant medical problems, if any. While there is reason for concern about the health of any child being adopted, the idea that there is a significantly higher incidence of serious illness in international adoption is not accurate.

In fact, there are some valid arguments that present the opposite viewpoint, based on our American lifestyle. Frank and his wife Ann adopted twice, once domestically and once internationally. "We did an international adoption the second time partly because of our own comfort level . . . we didn't feel comfortable talking with birth mothers, so we went overseas. We adopted from Latin America . . . and had excellent health information about the prenatal care taken by the birth mother. Having stayed very involved in the adoption community over the past fifteen years, I have realized that often there are more health problems inherent in domestic adoption. Our lifestyle (as Americans) is one that can lead to poorer prenatal care than that of some other countries where drugs and alcohol are not as prevalent. I'm not saying that birth mothers as a group abuse drugs or alcohol, only that it is much more common in our society as a whole. Any young person can be in a stressful situation and fall into these bad habits. Even our diet can be rich in junk foods. It is part of our lifestyle in this country and it does affect the prenatal care of a child. In a country such as China, Korea, or some South American countries, a birth mother does not have the same access to all of these things.

"Often, effects are found much later on in the child's life. We've heard of a number of circumstances where adoptive parents have discovered psychological and physical disorders that are traced back to poor prenatal care by birth mothers here in the United States."

The points raised in Frank's arguments are valid. The American lifestyle can be cause for concern. Today, however, greater communication between birth parents and adoptive parents can help to address such issues. Medical testing can provide greater insight into the prenatal health of the baby. But the birth mother has to be honest with the adoptive parents and amenable to providing such information or undergoing medical tests.

Contact with Birth Parents

Contact with birth parents is the other key issue that factors into the decision-making process. There is a wide range of theories regarding openness in adoption, or the involvement of birth parents in the adoptive child's (and adoptive parent's) life. The level of "openness" can vary from adoptive and birth families simply having specific contact information in case there is a need (such as medical) to reach each other, to ongoing involvement after the adoption has been finalized. . . . It is highly unlikely that you will have an open adoption with the birth parents of a child born internationally. Some people will see this as more comforting while others will find this far more distressing. . . .

Couples and singles must consider when approaching the process whether or not they will feel comfortable interacting with birth mothers at any level. Independent domestic adoption or agency-identified adoptions (two very common methods of domestic adoption) will require that adoptive parents talk with birth mothers to set up an adoption plan. In nearly 60 percent of domestic-adoption scenarios, the adoptive and birth parents meet in person. This is completely opposite in international adoption, where parental rights have been severed and birth parents and adoptive parents do not meet. For some people, meeting birth mothers is a wonderful part of the process but for others it becomes a roadblock.

According to New York/New Jersey–based adoption attorney Robin Fleischner;

> Contact with a birth mother can be a big plus in domestic adoption. It can result in being able to attain important medical records that are valuable in your child's future. It can also be a wonderful experience. Birth parents are not the enemy, they're working on a plan out of love to give the child a better life than they could provide. Once you've talked with them, you'll be able to share more with your child, having gotten to know the birth mother and possibly even the birth father. The fear people have is that they will go through this process with the birth mother, get very emotionally attached and then she'll decide to parent the child herself. This can be difficult emotionally, but it's still worth the risk. Most adoptive parents find that the positives of this relationship with a birth mother outweigh the negatives. Also, psychologists feel the more information parents have the better it is for themselves and for their children. . . .

Newborn or Older Child

What constitutes an "older child"? This depends on whom you are talking to. An older child can be a three-month-old, a toddler, or a five-, six-, or even twelve-year-old. Essentially, it is not a newborn baby. . . .

A newborn baby brings little or no emotional baggage along because his or her journey through life has been brief. As we grow, we all accumulate more emotional baggage. A child in foster care or in an orphanage is not growing up with the same ongoing sense of love and security as a child growing up in a healthy family environment.

Adopting an older child quite simply means the child will have more emotional issues to deal with. He or she is already aware of the outside world and what it has or has not had to offer. Generally speaking, the younger the child, the easier it is to overcome such issues. A one-year-old coming from an orphanage in another country will often have attachment disorders that love and patience can overcome. A four-year-old with behavioral problems will need more than just love. It will take a consistent effort and some work on your part to change negative behavioral problems. In many instances, it will require outside help. An older child (over two) will also ask questions about the transition in his or her life. You need to be prepared and well versed in how to deal with such questions. . . .

Gary and Fran's Case

Gary and Fran had adopted three times, through independent domestic placement, each time a newborn baby. Life was hectic for a two-income family with three children plus the obligatory pets, but like most families, they had settled into a steady routine—until they got an unexpected phone call. A friend they had known for several years through an adoption support group in which they had remained quite active, was calling with a most interesting situation. It seemed that she had been called by an adoption agency that was looking to place a domestic-born three-year-old girl. The agency, far more accustomed to dealing with the more common adoption of newborn domestic infants, or international adoptions of young children from orphanages abroad, was in a quandary trying to figure out whether or not they could find a home for this little girl. The child's birth mother did not want her in an institutionalized program such as the foster-care system but instead wanted to find a permanent loving family for her daughter whom she could not take care of.

"Apparently, the birth mother and birth father had split up. She was young and ill prepared to take care of her alone—and he was unable to take her with him. They felt that the best thing they could do was place her in a permanent loving home," Gary explains.

"My wife and I had talked about a fourth child, possibly through international adoption, but we had not acted on it in any way. I had just returned to night school, my wife was working, and we had three children, a nine-year-old and two eight-year-olds. We knew it was not going to be easy, but after discussing it, we decided to pursue the situation."

Gary and Fran started off slowly, visiting with young Debbie for a few hours. "We met with Debbie's birth mother and at first the birth father was not at all in the picture. The first few meetings went well. Finally we had a visit where we brought her out to the house for the day. She had a great time, she was very energetic, and the other kids loved having her around . . . I called it the 'new toy syndrome.' This was the first of what turned out to be a few visits. Then, when she would leave she would get hysterical and not want to go, which made us feel good that she was having fun but was also troubling because she was leaving with her birth mother."

As it turned out, Debbie had spent time living with her grandparents in Arizona and with her birth father, who later appeared in the picture. Apparently neither of them was ready for the responsibility of raising a child, so Gary and Fran adopted Debbie. "It took us a little time to get back into the mind-set of having a three-year-old around. For us it had been some time, and she needed much more constant attention than the older kids."

There were other issues that Gary and Fran needed to address that they had not dealt with when adopting previously. "We had psychologists and social workers meet her, and we talked with the board of health to find out about early-intervention programs and see what services she would be eligible for. She had some speech problems, among other things. We went through two or three weeks of evaluations. The psychologists and other people who saw her considered her 'bouncy.' No one wanted to label her as hyper or anything like that, so they kept using the term 'bouncy.' She clearly was not ADHD [Attention Deficit Hyperactivity Disorder] but it was best for her to have a special preschool program and some therapy."

Gary and Fran did not get much troubling behavior from Debbie. "We had been forewarned to expect bad behavior from an older child, but we didn't really get any—she was craving stability. The first couple of times she didn't behave, we put her in a time out and that was about it. She did test us a little bit, like if we were at the park she would take off and run out of the park and head down the street. Then she saw that we would always come after her, and she stopped doing it. For the most part she adjusted to everything very well. Our older kids needed time to adjust. The 'new toy syndrome' wore off after a few weeks, and they wondered why she was getting all the attention. It came and went with the two boys, but my older daughter needed a little more time to adjust now that she wasn't the only girl."

Now a family of six, things are hectic and busy around the house for Gary and Fran. Nonetheless, they have settled into a family routine once again. Gary does recommend that if you are bringing an older child into your home to be ready to deal with the child's life up to that point, which you will learn from him or her. In addition, if you have other children, expect that they, too, will need some time to adjust.

Open or Closed Adoption

"Open adoption" is generally defined as maintaining an open line of communication between the adoptive parents and the birth mother or birth parents after the adoption has been finalized. Nothing is set in stone when determining how much contact or communication constitutes an open adoption.

For many years, nearly all adoptions were done through agencies and were completely closed. Birth parents and adoptive parents had no communication before or after placement. Over the past twenty years, birth mothers have understandably wanted greater involvement in the placement of their children. Today they have a much greater say. Communication between birth parents and prospective adoptive parents prior to placement has become more commonplace with the growth of independent domestic placement. Over the past decade, there has also been an increase in maintaining the lines of communication after placement between birth and adoptive parents—or open adoption. . . .

Proponents of open adoption believe that it is beneficial to children because it gives them a better understanding of their biological roots and history. It gives children a sense of where they come from and what they will look like as adults. It helps paint a realistic picture of the birth parents and helps the adoptee to understand why he or she was placed for adoption, thus filling a void. It is also very helpful for knowledge about their medical history.

Open adoption allows birth parents to see how the child grows up and is raised. It lets them know firsthand how the child's life is turning out. From a birth mothers' perspective, she can also let the child and adoptive parents see her own life progression so that the child can know that the birth mother who was once unable to care for a child is now at a far more enhanced place in her life as well.

The adoptive parents can benefit by having some help in answering the tough adoption questions. They, too, can see what the child will be like when he or she grows up, both physically and emotionally.

Problems with Open Adoption

On the other side of the open-adoption argument, is the likelihood that a child, as he or she gets older, will not fully understand who mommy and daddy really are. Two sets of parents may be in the picture, yet they may very likely *not* agree on many issues and may have differing lifestyles. Children need a sense of consistency, stability, and one loving family. This can become very cloudy if another party is overly involved. Whereas a nineteen-, twenty- or twenty-one-year-old may be in a far more mature position to understand meeting his or her birth parents, a young child will not necessarily understand the situation. This can cause greater doubt or hurt when confronted often with the person who "gave them up for adoption" (using the words that the child might say). It can also be the root of greater emotional problems. . . .

Often a birth mother is either a teenager or a young woman without much money or emotional support. If she becomes overly dependent on the adoptive family, that, too, can cloud the issue, because you are not adopting her as well. She may feel that by remaining involved she can be a "backseat" parent, and this can become an unhealthy situation for all members of the triad.

In many cases, a birth mother wants to move on with her own life, which means she wants very much to make a clean separation for the sake of her emotional well-being and for the sake of the child and the adoptive parents. Proponents of open adoption often complain that too many adoptive parents are looking to take the child and get away quickly from the birth parents. Often, however, it is the birth mother who is looking to make a clean break. She has just made the toughest decision of her life and needs to separate for her own stability. It may be essential for her to move forward and get on with her life. This may necessitate a comfortable distance.

For adoptive parents, the desire for a closed adoption can help close the door on ambiguity over who is parenting and raising the child. It can help secure the family as a unit, providing a stable and loving environment for the child. This does not mean denying the child's right to know and understand adoption. It just may mean allowing a child to mature and grow in a stable family environment without such complications that he or she may be too young to assimilate into life's big picture.

CHAPTER 2

INTERNATIONAL ADOPTION

Contemporary Issues
Companion

INTERNATIONAL ADOPTION IS RISKY

Kim Clark and Nancy Shute

As the supply of babies available for adoption in the United States has plummeted since the mid–twentieth century, reporters Kim Clark and Nancy Shute say that an increasing number of Americans are looking abroad to adopt. Another reason international adoptions are becoming more popular, the authors say, is the fact that unregulated domestic adoption agencies and unscrupulous birthparents leave open the possibility of fraud and failed adoption agreements. But international adoptions are not without risks and pains either, as the authors state. For example, there are significant issues of bureaucracy, since the legal requirements of two different countries must be satisfied. Furthermore, Clark and Shute note that it is often impossible to know the health of children adopted from foreign countries, since many foreign nations have poor medical systems and underfunded orphanages. The costs of international adoptions also can be staggering, especially when travel expenses are taken into consideration. Kim Clark is a senior writer for *U.S. News & World Report*, and Nancy Shute is a freelance writer based in the Washington, D.C., area.

What longing is strong enough to pull a person halfway around the globe for a rendezvous with a stranger? It drew Barbara and Randy Combs from their home in Frederick, Md., to a Siberian winter 12 time zones away. On February 21 [2001], they stood in Novosibirsk's Baby Home No. 2, looking for the first time at 9-month-old Viktoria Istomina, who stared solemnly back. The moment was oddly quiet, considering that it would change all their lives forever. "In the photos she had brown eyes," Barbara said, "but they're beautiful blue, blue-gray." Randy petted the child's back. "Look at that!" he said. "When you smiled, it pretty much made my day."

The Combses are among the tens of thousands of Americans who decide each year to adopt a child. Barbara, a 41-year-old accountant, and Randy, a 42-year-old computer systems engineer, had anticipated producing a sibling for their 3-year-old daughter, Jordyn. But a ruptured ectopic pregnancy that almost killed Barbara last February made that impossible. "I wasn't sure about adoption," Barbara says, "but Randy had no qualms whatsoever." By summer's end, Barbara had laid to rest her fear that she would favor her biological child over an adopted one. They knew right away they were going to Russia; friends had just adopted from there, Barbara's family had Russian roots, and she was convinced that no American birth mother would ever pick them, because they were over 40 and already had a child. "There are children out there," Barbara said. "Let's do it."

Growing Social Acceptance and Rising Costs

In the past 35 years, adoption has been transformed from a shameful family secret to a praiseworthy act—one that finds families for children, helps birthparents in desperate straits, and brings the blessing of parenthood to the childless. Because of rising infertility rates and increasing societal acceptance of gay and single parents, interest in adoption has skyrocketed. A survey of American women in 1988 found just 200,000 considering adoption. By 1995, the last year for which statistics are available, 500,000 wanted to adopt a child. But most want a healthy white infant, and the supply of those has plummeted. As a result, the number of Americans heading overseas to build their families has more than doubled in the past decade to more than 18,000 a year.

But just as society has become more accepting of adoption, the process has become more difficult, expensive, and potentially heartbreaking. Adoption has moved from the tightly self-regulated realm of social-service agencies and unwed mothers' homes to the free market. Babies are hawked on Web sites that trumpet "FEES REDUCED" for individuals such as Child No. 678, "deformed right hand but mentally fine and very sweet." Hundreds of for-profit businesses and unlicensed facilitators promise to connect prospective parents with the child of their dreams—with costs ranging from $15,000 to $50,000. "I used to say adoption has become a business," says Susan Soon-keum Cox, a vice president with Holt International Children's Services in Eugene, Ore. "Now I say it's become an industry.". . .

The discrepancy between supply and demand has escalated adoption prices. Total spending on adoption is rising at 15 percent a year, hitting $1.4 billion in 2000. Although the Nebraska Children's Home Society provides free adoptions to state residents, most private domestic adoptions run from $6,000 to $30,000. Foreign adoptions run higher, starting at $15,000 for China to well over $20,000 for Guatemala. Randy and Barbara Combs figure it will have cost them $25,000 to $30,000 to adopt Viktoria, once travel costs are included. By far the biggest chunk, the $14,000 foreign fee, went to Frank Foundation Child Assistance International, a Washington, D.C.–based organization that is one of the largest locating children in Russia. In 1998, Frank made a profit of $937,515 on revenues of $4.1 million. Co-founder Nina Kostina earned $197,017. Many adoptive parents are deeply troubled by the vast sums of money they pay and the lack of accountability: "On Sunday I fly into Moscow with $12,000 in cash strapped to my person," says Karen Groth, a 37-year-old Air Force major and intelligence officer who's adopting a baby girl from Kazakhstan. "Where does all our money go?". . .

What Drives Americans to Look Abroad

Prospective parents have few legal safeguards. Government officials [in America] rarely treat their complaints [about domestic adoptions] seriously. Bill Lee, Maryland's adoption licensing coordinator, says when he gets complaints from adoptive parents about money, he makes a courtesy investigative phone call but can do nothing more: "We toss 'em." The state's regulations don't cover such contract disputes, he explains. Other officials move, but glacially. In a lawsuit, Candy and Bob Murdock, a Georgia couple, allege they paid $11,000 in 1998 to Lorraine Boisselle, who ran a Mississippi adoption agency. Two years later, after they say Boisselle gave them increasingly outlandish explanations for her failure to find a child (she once blamed a hurricane), the Murdocks called the Mississippi attorney general's office. They say they were surprised to learn that there were already complaints pending and that Boisselle's license had lapsed. The state says it is still investigating Boisselle. The Murdocks have joined with two other victims in filing a civil suit in an attempt to recover their money. "There is no way you can protect yourself," Candy Murdock says. After her experience, "I would tell anybody considering adoption to go international."

That's precisely what many people are deciding to do. [In the 1990s], the number of children adopted from overseas has more than doubled, from 7,093 in 1990 to 18,441 [in 2000], and the numbers are expected to keep rising. Foreign adoption became institutionalized in the 1950s after the Korean War, when Americans began adopting orphans and Amerasian children. But the picture radically changed in the early 1990s. Images of gruesome Romanian orphanages sparked an international effort to rescue children there. The fall of communism in the Soviet bloc paved the way for adoption from Russia and its former republics. And China started allowing foreign adoption of the thousands of girls abandoned by a society that favors male offspring. China and Russia have now eclipsed South Korea as the top two sources of foreign adoptions in the United States, with Guatemala a close fourth. Hundreds of new agencies have sprung up to meet this increased demand.

But foreign adoption, even if it avoids some of the complications of domestic adoption, brings its own difficulties. Two countries' legal requirements must be met, two bureaucracies assuaged. "I applied for a job at the CIA once," Randy Combs recalls. "This was much more paperwork." All adoptions require a home study. Going international requires a dossier of documents for the foreign country and approval by the U.S. Immigration and Naturalization Service. Deanna Hodgin and Philip Dworsky have waited four months for INS approval of their petition to adopt an infant girl from Kazakhstan. Hodgin, a San Francisco communications manager, says she'll quit her job in mid-March and fly to Kazakhstan and wait there: "At least while I'm there I can see the baby each day, feed her some more-nutritious food, and try to improve her condition."

Health Guesswork

The most daunting, and potentially devastating, hurdle in international adoption is assessing a child's health in the face of incomplete or faulty medical information. Nobody wants to go through what Debbie and David Crick of Apison, Tenn., have. They adopted a boy they thought was 10 years old from the Republic of Georgia in 1996, only to find out he was actually 14 and seriously mentally ill. In the case of Randy and Barbara Combs, the couple know nothing about their daughter's birth father and little more about her birth mother, a 20-year-old shop clerk who left the newborn at the maternity hospital. Prospective parents typically receive a short video of a child and a synopsis of the medical history. Little Viktoria's analysis included neurological terms like "pyramidal insufficiency" and "perinatal encephalopathy." "It's very scary," says Barbara. The Combses took their video and report to a pediatrician, and also called the orphanage's doctor with the help of a translator. "She's good kind baby," the doctor said. The couple started packing for Siberia.

Most children coming to the United States are from countries like Russia with poor medical systems, where pregnant women often get no prenatal care and are malnourished. Children adopted from abroad also often suffer ailments that a suburban pediatrician wouldn't even think to look for, including syphilis, tuberculosis, intestinal parasites, and hepatitis B and C.

Those health problems are exacerbated in orphanages, where children are often underfed and the lack of individual attention delays physical and mental development. In a study published in 2000, 75 percent of children adopted from China had significant developmental delays. (Korea and Guatemala are considered exceptions, because children are placed in foster care instead of in orphanages and usually get good medical care.) "These kids are high risk," says Ronald Federici, an Alexandria, Va., neuropsychologist who treats foreign adoptees. Many agencies, he says, require parents to sign liability waivers, which absolve the agency of responsibility if the child later turns out to have serious medical or psychological problems.

Indeed, Frank Foundation's Nina Kostina says that parents need to be ready to bail out: "When the parents are in the orphanage with the medical records in front of them, this is the time. Call your pediatrician in the United States. This is a lifetime decision."

Given the emotional investment, that's not easy. Barbara Combs says she doesn't think she would have had the strength to say no once she'd made it all the way to Novosibirsk, after an overnight flight from Moscow. Fortunately, she felt she didn't have to. The medical information from the orphanage doctor matched what she'd heard before, aside from a "peculiarity of the coccyx." The translator started dictating a letter to the court, as Randy wrote longhand: "We have met the child and bonded with her. We are aware of her health concerns."

Heading Home

Two days later, Barbara and Randy were standing before a Siberian judge, who after 40 minutes of questions declared that Viktoria Nikolaevna Istomina was now Victoria Nicole Combs. Three days later, the sleep-deprived family was on the plane for home, surrounded by other adoptive parents with wailing babies. Victoria was diagnosed with a mild case of rickets due to lack of vitamin D, and her family doctor said the "peculiarity of the coccyx" dismissed by the orphanage doctor may require surgery. But her exhausted parents remain pleased. "Considering you're going to another country and taking guardianship of another human being," Randy says, "it's been amazingly smooth."

In March 2001, Victoria made history as she and about 75,000 other children adopted from abroad instantly became American citizens, thanks to the Childhood Citizenship Act of 2000, designed so that foreign adoptees would not risk being deported if their parents failed to have them naturalized. Children adopted abroad now become citizens once they enter the States. That, and . . . legislation that [raised] the federal tax credit for adoption from $5,000 to $10,000 per child, are hailed by adoptive parents and advocates as significant steps toward encouraging adoption. The third step is more significant still—the Hague Convention on Intercountry Adoption. [In 2000], after a decade of effort, Congress approved legislation to implement the international treaty, which is designed to stop trafficking in children and promote international adoption. For the first time, the United States will have a central authority that will accredit adoption agencies and a federal database. "If there are enough complaints about an agency, that agency could be removed," says Mary Marshall, director of the office of children's issues at the State Department. It will take up to three years for the central authority to be created, but once it's online, prospective parents will have for the first time a central source of information on agencies, one that should prove useful to parents adopting domestically as well.

In the meantime, adoption advocates say parents should use their heads, not just their hearts, when seeking a child. "If you were buying a car, you wouldn't plunk down your $45,000 without looking it up in *Consumer Reports*," says Jerri Jenista, an Ann Arbor, Mich., pediatrician who has been practicing adoption medicine for 20 years and who has adopted five children from India. "I see people who adopt a child for the same amount of money with zero preparation. You have to do your homework."

THE HAGUE TREATY CAN REMOVE SOME OF THE RISKS OF INTERNATIONAL ADOPTION

Ethan B. Kapstein

The market forces of supply and demand will always exist in international adoptions as long as children languish in orphanages in some parts of the world and families long to adopt in other parts of the world, says scholar and writer Ethan B. Kapstein. In the following article, Kapstein claims that the "baby market" has led to corrupt adoption networks that traffic in children who have been sold or kidnapped. To combat the exploitation of children, the international community has constructed a legal framework to encourage international adoption when a child's best interest is served and to prevent illicit trade in children, Kapstein states. A treaty called the Hague Convention on the Protection of Children and Cooperation in Respect of Intercountry Adoption has been the fruit of this international effort. Kapstein argues that the convention should be widely implemented and that more funding should be made available to ensure the success of its aims. Kapstein is a professor of sustainable development at a French academy.

Children are our most precious resource—and, like most precious resources, they are traded across borders. As more parents have adopted babies from abroad [since the early 1990s], the international market for children has boomed: in 2001, some 34,000 children—mainly from Asia and central and eastern Europe—found new homes in western Europe and North America.

With 9.5 million children now languishing in developing-world orphanages, there are many more opportunities to create loving families across borders. Yet, because the demand for infants from poor countries is rising among adults who live in wealthy ones, corruption has distorted the baby trade. Unscrupulous go-betweens buy or abduct infants from needy biological parents and sell them to eager adoptive families.

Facilitating the placement of orphaned children while attacking the corruption that accompanies it will be a fine balancing act. A free market for babies is out of the question: while infants can fetch a high price, they are not, and should never be treated as, commodities. But banning adoptions from countries that tolerate corrupt adoption rings is no solution either. Moratoriums have been imposed on adoptions from Cambodia and Romania, for example, but they only succeeded in denying orphans there a chance to find families while shifting the demand to new suppliers such as Russia and China.

A more promising course would be to reinforce the multilateral legal regime that regulates global adoption. The Hague Convention on Protection of Children and Cooperation in Respect of Intercountry Adoption, now in force in 54 countries, requires states to facilitate international adoptions while stamping out exploitation. Strengthening this regime is essential to the well-being of orphans and to the parents who would receive them. But doing so will require more diplomatic pressure, more foreign aid, and more political courage in confronting traffickers than the international community has yet mustered.

Baby Boom

Historically, international adoption has sprouted in the aftermath of wars. After World War II, American families adopted European orphans, chiefly from Germany, Italy, and Greece; after the war in Korea, they took in children from that devastated peninsula. At the end of the Vietnam conflict in 1975, some 3,000 children were adopted by foreign parents as part of Operation Babylift. So many infants left Vietnam that in 1983, Hanoi declared a moratorium on further adoptions, which has since been lifted.

More recently, changes in economic and social policies have determined the sources of supply. With the end of the Cold War, market-driven economics were ushered into central and eastern Europe, causing the collapse of communist-era welfare systems and a surge in the number of abandoned children. Romania, for example, had allowed only 30 intercountry adoptions in 1989; in the year after the fall of [dictator] Nicolae Ceausescu, it let more than 10,000 children leave the country.

Likewise, although no Russian child was adopted abroad prior to 1990, Russia is now the world's largest supplier of orphans to parents in the United States, satisfying about 40 percent of total demand. China, which also frowned on giving up its orphans for international adoption in the late 1980s, now ranks as a close second. Its one-child policy, which strongly favors boys, has left many Chinese girls in need of foreign parents. In fact, it is estimated that two-thirds of all children put up for adoption are female.

At the same time, the demand for foreign-born babies has soared in the West, thanks largely to changing social norms, such as increasingly relaxed notions of what constitutes a family. As couples wait longer to marry and, as a result, have fewer children of their own, many more seek to create families through adoption. So do an increasing number of single adults and gay couples.

Prospective parents today have a more difficult time finding babies at home, because relatively fewer children born in Western countries are now put up for adoption. In the United States, for example, adoptions of U.S.-born children satisfy between one-half and two-thirds of the total demand for nonbiological children. (Precise figures are difficult to compile because the U.S. government—like many others—does not keep very reliable statistics.)

A Global Business

The combined effect of these social and economic changes has been a boom in the international adoption trade. Between 1988 and 2001, the number of cross-border adoptions nearly doubled, jumping from about 19,000 to over 34,000. By 2001, Americans alone accounted for 19,237 international adoptions—over half of the world's total. Other industrial states have recorded even more spectacular increases: in Canada, the number climbed from 232 to 1,874 between 1988 and 2001; in Spain, it skyrocketed from a mere 93 to 3,428 in the same period.

The baby trade is likely to continue to grow, partly because it is no longer simply a response to wars and humanitarian crises. For better or worse, it now behaves much like a commodities market, with demand informing supply; and neither demand nor supply is likely to subside. As the HIV/AIDS pandemic grows, many more babies will become available for adoption around the world. Some 13 million children already have lost one or both parents to AIDS. According to UNICEF, that number is projected to reach 25 million by 2010. Most of these children live in sub-Saharan African countries, which have not traditionally been an important source for international adoptions because of cultural and religious strictures on that practice. But this reluctance could wane as the AIDS crisis mounts, if extended families can no longer function as caregivers. Some African countries, such as Ethiopia, are already becoming more open to international adoption. As AIDS spreads throughout eastern Europe and Asia, the number of orphans will surely grow in these regions also—as will the challenge of finding new homes for them.

Growing Pains

International adoptions were largely unregulated until the 1980s and 1990s, when several appalling trafficking stories made headlines in international media, prompting political action. The most widespread and alarming problem has been the illicit purchase and sale of babies. From Albania to India, families and orphanages have swapped children for money, television sets, cameras, or watches. [An] article in *The New*

York Times revealed that a family in India sold their month-old daughter for $20 to a "woman from a nearby village," who then sold the baby to an orphanage, which in turn arranged for its adoption abroad.

In the worst cases, infants are sold after having been abducted. Some of the most egregious examples of that practice have emerged from Central America. Senior officials in Honduras allegedly helped kidnap children from poor families and sell them to foreigners in the early 1990s. A 2000 report by the United Nations found that in Guatemala, a leading supplier of infants worldwide, "in the majority of cases, international adoption involve[s] a variety of criminal offences, including the buying and selling of children, the falsifying of documents, the kidnapping of children, and the housing of (these) babies awaiting private adoption."

Stopping this traffic will be no small feat. The basic economic incentives that rule markets have a powerful hold, even when the trade is for humans. Infants can fetch anywhere between $5,000 and $25,000. Even if the biological parents see only a small fraction of that amount, in impoverished countries that may be a hefty sum. And parents in receiving countries buy babies in spite of corruption, in the hope of giving them a better life, without realizing that they may be encouraging more trafficking.

It is also difficult at times to distinguish child trafficking from legitimate adoption; the difference may be clear conceptually, but it is not always clear in reality. An American agency that helped bring 600 Russian children to the United States in the 1990s admitted giving orphanages clothing and medical supplies in order to establish preferential relationships with them. But the agency claimed that because it did not pay the orphanages, the Russians had not been "selling the children." Buying infants is illegal; covering the cost of raising them until they are adopted is not. The distinction between the two can be so obscure, however, that unless parents actually confess to selling their children, adoption and immigration authorities may struggle to prove it.

The discovery of corrupt practices has prompted some receiving states to ban adoptions from suppliers with sketchy records and some suppliers to suspend the emigration of orphans while they review their own practices. These moratoriums only displace the problem, however: sanctions against some countries simply shift the market to new suppliers. The number of Romanians available for international adoption seesawed throughout the 1990s and 2000s, as moratoriums were imposed and repealed and imposed again while the Romanian government wrestled with charges of corruption. In 2001, Romania placed 782 children in the United States; the following year, with another moratorium in place, the number dropped to 168. During the same period, adoptions in the United States of children from Russia increased by about 700, and adoptions of children from China increased by about 350. The shift in suppliers shows that unilateral or bilateral measures cannot be effective means of regulating a trade that, by definition, affects thousands of children and scores of countries. A single adoption may involve several jurisdictions: a child born in Malaysia may be adopted in Singapore by parents living in Ireland who seek to bring the child home through the United Kingdom.

Baby Steps Toward Regulation

Recognizing these shortcomings, in the late 1980s, the UN [United Nations] launched multilateral discussions to develop a normative framework for the baby trade. (Earlier attempts to regulate the baby trade had been made at the regional level, in the Americas, western Europe, and the Nordic countries, but given the international nature of this commerce, they had proved ineffective.) Negotiations culminated in the adoption of the Convention on the Rights of the Child (CRC) in 1989. The CRC distinguishes child trafficking from legitimate adoptions, stating that the placement of children should not result "in improper financial gain for those involved in it." The convention also states that "intercountry adoption may be considered as an alternative means of a child's care, if the child cannot be placed in a foster or an adoptive family or cannot in any suitable manner be cared for in the child's country of origin."

The CRC was an important but tentative first step toward regulating international adoption. The convention does not define "improper financial gain," for example, offering no guidelines for telling bribes apart from acceptable child support. Also, the convention's preference for in-country solutions over intercountry adoption places the onus on home countries to clean up their orphanage and adoption systems. That, however, has proved beyond the capabilities of most states, particularly those in the developing world. The temptations of profitable cross-border transactions give these countries little incentive to encourage adoptions at home, especially when they often lack the resources to fund such efforts in the first place.

The Hague Convention

The CRC itself does not regulate international adoption. But it directs the 191 states that are party to it to conclude "multilateral arrangements or agreements" to establish a transparent process for adopting children across national borders, including by passing necessary legislation at home. That challenge was taken up by the Hague Conference on Private International Law, a little-known intergovernmental organization created in 1893 and tasked with unifying the rules of private international law. In 1993, the conference presented to its member countries a draft convention on international adoption, which they promptly and unanimously endorsed.

Now in force in 54 countries and signed, but awaiting ratification, by another nine, the Hague Convention on Protection of Children and Cooperation in Respect of Intercountry Adoption is the baby trade's legal backbone. Heeding the CRC's call, the Hague Convention seeks "to take measures to ensure that intercountry adoptions are made in the best interests of the child and with respect for his or her fundamental rights, and to prevent the abduction, the sale of, or traffic in children."

Whereas the CRC states that children should remain in their home country so long as foster care can be found there, under the Hague Convention intercountry adoption is acceptable if a "suitable family" cannot be found in a child's home state. In other words, the two documents are informed by opposite presumptions: the Hague Convention snubs the CRC's preference for domestic solutions, holding instead that the "best interests of the child" may be better served by a foreign adoptive family than by a domestic orphanage.

The Hague Convention also aims to establish a "system of cooperation" among states to prevent the traffic in children. It recognizes that child trafficking, like terrorism and the drug trade, can only be curbed through multilateral cooperation. (The international police authority Interpol was an active participant in the Hague Convention's deliberations.)

Home Country Control

Finally, the Hague Convention requires that states amend their national adoption laws to conform to the convention's principles and guidelines. The terms of the convention require both supplying and receiving countries to implement new legislation: it asks the first to clean up corrupt adoption networks, and the second to crack down on the receipt of trafficked children. The children's country of origin must also certify that they are in fact legally adoptable.

This feature, which could be called "home country control," was a necessary compromise. It was the product of negotiations among the convention's participants, who came from different backgrounds and held radically different views concerning adoption. Islam, for example, strictly prohibits adoption, although it does permit a type of fosterparenting arrangement. In India, only Hindus are allowed to adopt Hindu children, as several American families painfully discovered recently when Indian courts barred them from adopting local children. The Hague Convention reflects the need to let states legislate these issues internally, consistent with their values. That flexibility was all the more important given that adoption legislation is relatively undeveloped in most countries and jurists are struggling to define the legal relationship between adopted children and their biological parents, their adoptive parents, and their siblings.

A key feature of the Hague Convention, therefore, is its requirement that each state designate a "central authority" to oversee the adoption process in its own territory, including the implementation of the convention's directives through new domestic legislation and the coordination of adoption procedures with other states. The difficulty of this task cannot be underestimated, especially in federal countries such as the United States, where adoption is the prerogative of individual states rather than the national government. Three years after the Intercountry Adoption Act of 2000 was passed by Congress and signed into law by President Bill Clinton, regulations to implement the Hague Convention in the United States are still forthcoming. The delay has generated tension between Congress and the State Department, the United States' designated central authority.

Room for Growth

The Hague Convention is rightly seen as a major breakthrough: it holds that the best interests of children should guide any effort to regulate adoptions; it favors international adoptions over resort to domestic orphanages; and it streamlines the adoption process by requiring that supplying states certify children who may be adopted. Therefore, extending and enforcing the convention should become a priority.

As the country that adopts most foreign children, the United States should hurry to implement it. [According to the U.S. Department of State, it is hoped that preparations for implementation of the Convention will permit the United States to bring it into force by early 2006.] Washington should also exert diplomatic pressure on major supplying states—such as Cambodia, Haiti, Kazakhstan, South Korea, Ukraine, and Vietnam—that have not yet become parties to the convention. The European Union [EU] also has a key role to play in this respect. As active participants in the baby trade seek membership or free trade agreements with the EU, they will become increasingly susceptible to Brussels' moral suasion. The EU should tie any ongoing economic negotiations with countries involved in the baby trade to improvements in their adoption practices.

Despite its contributions, however, the Hague Convention regime does not, and cannot, tackle systemic corruption, which is likely to worsen as the trade in foreign-born children increases. One of the convention's limitations is precisely the discretion it leaves states to regulate their own adoption networks; "home country control" does little to curb the corruption that is endemic in some places. If poorly paid officials will take payoffs to fix parking tickets or facilitate foreign direct investment, how can it be assumed that they will not take cuts on child trafficking?

Even in the cleanest of supplier states, there is little money to spare for tracking abuses, funding orphanages, or supporting educational and health care services. It is essential, therefore, that aid be granted to states that need but cannot afford to reinforce their child welfare systems. That goes for states that have not signed the Hague Convention too—perhaps even more so. As U.S. Congressman Henry Hyde, a leading advocate for intercountry adoption, has pointed out, "some of the foreign countries whose systems are the most problematic are unlikely to ratify the Convention anytime soon." Very little foreign aid is currently earmarked for adoption and child welfare issues.

Improvements Can Be Made

More modest policies can also help, if only by simplifying existing adoption procedures and promoting goodwill. In 2002, the U.S. government launched a promising initiative, "Adjudicate Orphan Status First," to screen babies before prospective parents initiate lengthy and costly procedures to adopt them. Under this program, the Bureau of Citizenship and Immigration Services conducts nonbinding reviews of orphans in Poland, Sierra Leone, Haiti, Honduras, and the Philippines to determine whether they are in fact eligible for adoption and immigration to the United States. The program is designed to spare many families the pain of discovering that they cannot adopt the baby they cherish because of health problems, trafficking, or other irregularities. If the program proves to facilitate intercountry adoption by increasing transparency and predictability, it should be extended to other supplier states and appropriately funded by Congress.

Measures short of adoption that provide comfort to orphans should also be encouraged. Foster parenting, for example, allows a family to support financially an orphaned child from afar, often in the form of a monthly stipend. Unfortunately, potential foster parents are often reluctant to contribute to the upkeep of children who live in countries where the government, intermediary agencies, or orphanages are suspected of being mismanaged or unaccountable. Western governments, international organizations such as UNICEF and nongovernmental organizations could help dispel such concerns by providing better information about, and perhaps even certifying, institutions that would receive assistance. Governments should also subsidize the generosity of foster parents by offering them tax breaks, as many do for charitable contributions.

Turning the baby trade into an open market would do nothing to stamp out corruption and abuses; it may even encourage some women to breed children simply with the goal of selling them. So the course paved by the Hague Convention—a multilateral, forward-looking strategy—is the one to follow and to support with commonsense policies, diplomatic pressures, and, of course, adequate funding.

To be sure, our failure to build an effective international adoption regime is unlikely to dominate the foreign policy agenda these days; it threatens neither national security nor economic welfare. But with worldwide adoptions on the rise, it is a pressing problem nonetheless. Fixing it would help bring together the thousands of children and parents whose only desire is to build a family. In this day and age, that is no small achievement.

Transcultural Adoption Poses Unique Challenges to Families and Children

Anne Adams Lang

In the following article, reporter Anne Adams Lang writes that in the United States, international adoption most often means white parents will extend their family to include a child from a different racial or cultural group. Interracial, multicultural families are created seemingly overnight, Lang notes, and questions about the best way to raise children so that they are familiar and comfortable with both their birth and adoptive cultures are still being addressed. Some adoptive parents strive to learn about the countries and cultures of their adopted children so that they might assist in creating a link for their children to the countries of their birth. At the same time, Lang asserts, some adopted children struggle solely to assimilate and are bothered by the fact that they are seen as being different from their adoptive families because of their racial or ethnic appearances. Lang is a freelance writer, specializing in social and political issues.

She was 18 years old when it first happened. Hollee McGuiness went on a trip with her high school class, and her sense of self was assaulted. "I was walking through the airport with friends and someone stopped me and said, 'Sign this petition for your Korean country,'" she recalled. "I said, 'I'm American.'"

It happened again. This time, she was with the Caucasian family who adopted her when she was 3½ years old. "I kept wondering why people were asking me where I was from," she said. "They didn't see me as Hollee. They saw me as an Asian woman."

Questions of Identity

Identity crises are a birthright in the United States. We expect to be jolted by them throughout our lifetimes. As parents we instinctively brace for the eruptions of our children, who will spew questions about who and what they are like white-hot lava. Factor in adoption and the equation becomes more complicated. Pile on racial and cultural differences between parent and child, and the calculus is daunting.

"There are many of us who have struggled with our parents not matching who we are on the outside," said Joy Lieberthal, a 29-year-old Korean adoptee who is a policy analyst at the Evan D. Donaldson Adoption Institute in Manhattan, which researches adoption practices and policies. "It's about always being subjected by the public to justify our existence as a member of a family, a community and as an individual."

Though still just a small percentage of all adoptions in the United States (estimated at 100,000 to 120,000 a year), international adoptions are rising steadily, to 16,396 in 1999 from 7,093 in 1990. Most of those adoptive parents are white. In the 1999 fiscal year, Russia was the leading source country, with 4,348, followed by China, with 4,101, and South Korea, with 2,008, according to the Joint Council on International Adoption Services.

Domestic adoptions of African-Americans by white families, the subject of decades of controversy, occur in small numbers. There are no definitive numbers, but in 1995 the Child Welfare League of America estimated that 4 percent of all foster care adoptions were transracial.

The 1994 Multiethnic Placement Act and its 1996 amendment prohibit agencies from delaying or denying a child's placement on the basis of race, color or national origin. Recent court decisions favoring white adults' adopting black children may increase the numbers.

But the prevailing notion remains that same-race adoptions are ideal. "You have to keep this in context," said Janice Shindler, the acting executive director of the New York Chapter of the Association of Black Social Workers. "This is happening in a society in which race matters. Black families raising black children, by the very fact of having this common experience, impart knowledge, values and expectations to the children." Federal law even mandates that agencies recruit adoptive families from a child's ethnic and racial community.

Combining Cultures

That said, the desire of adults to have families means that transracial adoptions are going to be part of the landscape. What is less certain is how transracial adoptees should be raised. "Parents must understand that they're not white parents with a black or Asian child, but they've become an interracial and multicultural family," said Ronnie Diamond, the head of postadoption services at Spence-Chapin, a private agency in Manhattan with a large international program.

Spence-Chapin asks prospective adoptive parents to scrutinize their own attitudes. "We want to hear parents' willingness to help their children learn about their culture, heritage and racial issues," said Kathy Legg, the executive director. That means vetting the extended family for racist attitudes. It means living in an integrated neighborhood. It also means ensuring that children have role models of their own race and, often, that they take language lessons.

Susan Kellman, who is a criminal lawyer, lives in a mixed Brooklyn neighborhood with her biological son, Ben, 10, and her adopted Chinese daughter, Mia, 4. "It's uphill making the connection between Chinese culture and us by insisting on Chinese cooking or a Chinese New Year's banquet," Ms. Kellman said. "Mia is working as hard as she can to assimilate. All she wants to do is go to synagogue on Friday night."

Ms. Kellman, a single mother, trusts that her daughter instinctively knows what is right for her. "I don't push her to connect in a 'Chinese' sense," she said. "It's out there if she wants it. We go to Chinese art shows and celebrate the Autumn Moon. We do Chinese drawing. Ben and I are far more interested in that than she is. But she's 4. Who knows how she'll process all this?"

Other families go for total immersion, with Mandarin dancing lessons and Chinese schools. Some travel regularly to China.

"There is this idea that if you give a child a language or dancing lessons that will allow them to grow up with the identity they need as a cultural minority in this country," said Dr. Amanda Baden, a psychologist who teaches at St. John's University in New York. "That's not necessarily the case." There is the larger society and the experiences of the immediate family to contend with, said Dr. Baden, 31 and a Hong Kong adoptee. And there is no guarantee that the child will ever feel comfortable with his or her birth culture.

Transracial Adoptive Families

Then there is the matter of race, a thornier issue, said Dr. Baden and Dennis Bisgaard, who jointly teach a workshop on race, identity and adoption. "People who have never faced race relations close up, they adopt a child from a different racial group, and suddenly they have to confront their own biases and assumptions," said Mr. Bisgaard, who is a black-Caucasian adoptee and head of the diversity program at the Collegiate School, a private school in Manhattan. Mr. Bisgaard grew up in Germany and Denmark, in white cultures, and has lived in the United States for the last 12 years. "I am biracial, and at one point I aspired to being African-American," he said. "After being exposed to and often rejected by African-American culture, I had to make up my own identity. Now, I feel comfortable knowing I don't belong to any one group."

Race and genetic makeup, therefore, are only a part of one's identity. "Your core comprises any number of qualities," he said. "Like you might be gay or deeply religious." Nurturing that whole self requires a loving, secure home, he added.

In Sonoma County, Calif., Nancy Fogarty and Jim Henrikson, film-music editors, are bringing up their Mexican daughter, Alana, 14, in a predominantly white, rural setting. The area, they admit, is racially isolating. But Ms. Fogarty said, "Our job is to raise somebody who has the faculties to get what she needs." That includes understanding her heritage.

They expose Alana to Mexican art and music. A Mexican girl who lived with them for five years while attending school functioned as a kind of older sister. "As for racism, we can't pretend we know what it feels like because we don't know what it is to walk in her skin," Mr. Henrikson said. "But she's growing up in a house that won't tolerate prejudices in that regard."

Alana is acutely aware of race at times. "People say: 'Oh, is she your daughter? Cause you don't look the same,'" she said. "It bothers me that strangers feel like they can do that."

Transforming Stereotypes

Such incidents make her parents nervous about what the world might dish out. But there is now a generation of adult adoptees to point the way. "I raged about people seeing me as different," said Ms. McGuiness, who founded Also Known As, an organization of adult transracial adoptees. "One man told me he loved dating Asian women. He had assumptions about Asians. He also assumed that I wasn't really American because of the way I looked."

At 28, Ms. McGuiness, a computer consultant, has an ambitious goal—transforming racial stereotypes. After all, she said, "our very existence defies those stereotypes."

EXPORTING BLACK BABIES THROUGH FOREIGN ADOPTIONS

Dawn Davenport

An often overlooked aspect of international adoption is the number of babies born in America and adopted by families in other countries. The following selection by Dawn Davenport of the *Christian Science Monitor* examines possible reasons for why many American-born babies, predominantly African American, are placed with parents overseas even as U.S. couples increasingly adopt from abroad. Davenport is a contributor to the *Christian Science Monitor* and author of the forthcoming book *Finding a Child: The Complete Guide to International Adoption.*

Adrian Stokkeland, a 2-year-old in Canada, dances with his mom to the music of Elvis and sleeps with his most treasured possession, a box of toy cars. Emma Sonnenschein, an energetic 19-month-old in Germany, loves to "help" her mom around the house. Elisa van Meurs, a 5-year-old in the Netherlands, is a real girly-girl. Her favorite outfit is a Minnie Mouse dress, paired with a Snow White tiara and pink Barbie shoes.

Adrian, Emma, and Elisa have more in common than their charm and being the apple of their parents' eyes. All are black children born in the United States and adopted as infants by parents in other countries.

They also are representatives of a little-known trend: At the same time the US is "importing" increasing numbers of adoptive children from Russia, China, and Guatemala, it is "exporting" black babies to be adopted in other countries.

Since 1995, US State Department records indicate that international adoptions by Americans have increased more than 140 percent. Couples often cite the lack of American babies as the reason for adopting from abroad.

But the US is now the fourth largest "supplier" of babies for adoption to Canada. Adoption by Shepherd Care, an agency in Hollywood, Fla., places 90 percent of its African-American babies in Canada. One-third of the children placed through Adoption-Link in Chicago, which specializes in adoptions for black babies, go to people from other countries.

The exact numbers are not available, but interviews with adoption agencies and families in Canada, Germany, France, and the Netherlands indicate that the US also sends babies to those four countries as well as Belgium and England. Most of the children are black newborns. Most of the adopting parents are Caucasian.

Why Is It Happening?

There is no simple explanation for why many white Americans prefer to adopt from abroad rather than adopt the available black babies at home. Racism is one reason, says Cheryl Kinnaird of Adoption-Link in Chicago. But there are others, she adds.

Families might choose an international adoption because of an affinity for a particular country or a desire to help. Many couples want a child who resembles them so that their family will not stand out as an "adoptive family." Since most adoptive families are Caucasian, this might explain the rise in adoptions from Russia and other eastern European countries.

In 2003, 37 percent of all international adoptions to the US were from countries where the majority of children adopted were Caucasian.

White couples may also be concerned about how their extended family will react to a black child. And they sometimes worry they are not up to the task of raising a black child in America and are not sure it is in the best interest of the child to be raised in a white environment.

Then, too, whites often are uncertain whether they can provide the child with cultural exposure to the African-American community.

Most adoption professionals agree that, all other things being equal, it is best to place an African-American child with an African-American family. The National Association of Black Social Workers' position is that every effort should be made to place children with families of the same race and culture.

Most, but not all, birth mothers agree, if they have the choice. However, they do not often have the choice, since fewer African-American couples apply to adoption agencies. One reason is that babies are frequently available within their extended family or community, and they have no need to go through the expense of an agency to adopt. Also, the number of infertile black couples who can afford to adopt is simply not as large as the number of black babies available.

The Word Hasn't Gotten Out

Some speculate that African-American babies have lagged behind in adoption rates because many Americans don't realize they're available. Media coverage and popular culture have focused on Americans adopting internationally rather than domestically.

"When we started to think about adoption, we thought only of international adoption because that's all we were hearing about," says Lisa Malaquin-Prey of North Carolina, mother of an adopted Russian baby. "We thought it would cost too much and that we would have to wait for a long time if we adopted domestically."

"I think that more Americans would adopt these babies if they knew they were available," says Stacy Hyer, a white American living in Germany with two adopted black children.

There is evidence of increasing adoption of black babies by white American families. But ingrained preferences still play a part in who is chosen for adoption.

The majority of couples seeking to adopt are white, but there aren't nearly enough Caucasian babies available in the US to meet the demand. Although exceptions certainly exist, American parents generally prefer babies to toddlers, girls to boys, and Caucasians to African-Americans, adoption professionals report. Other ethnicities fall in between, depending on their skin color. African-American boys are at the bottom of this "ranking" system, they say, which is why they're harder to place.

"We have to work much harder to find homes for our African-American babies," says Robert Springer of Christian Homes, an adoption agency in Texas.

No one is equating babies with commodities, but the principles of supply and demand apply. Adoption costs and waiting times in the US vary depending on a baby's ranking in the "desirability list."

The children who are in the greatest demand are also in the shortest supply. Those who want to adopt healthy white babies in the US may wait as long as five years, agencies say. In contrast, they add, the waiting for African-Americans is often measured in weeks and months, especially for baby boys.

The demand for biracial (black/white) babies falls in between, and the wait reflects this. The waiting period for a biracial girl can be more than a year.

It's also the case that adopting a white baby costs more than adopting a black or biracial one.

Adoption fees for healthy Caucasian babies can be as high as $40,000, according to the US Department of Health and Human Services. For biracial babies, the cost is about $18,000. For African-American newborns, it ranges from $10,000 to $12,000, agencies say.

The costs to the adoption agency for each child also vary greatly, not because of race but due to circumstances. The agency may have paid all the prenatal expenses and living costs for one birth mother, for instance, and not another, who decided on adoption in her ninth month of pregnancy.

But instead of passing along the actual costs to the new parents, many adoption agencies—most of which are nonprofit—charge a set fee that is determined by how difficult the baby may be to place. The agencies say this enables them to find homes for the children who are hardest to place.

Fees and waiting times for American families adopting internationally vary by country, but total costs, including travel, are usually about $30,000, with a waiting time of nine to 18 months.

Because of regulations and laws in the country of origin, most of the foreign children adopted from abroad by Americans are more than 1 year old when they arrive in the US.

In contrast, American babies can be adopted as soon as their parents relinquish them.

Families in foreign countries cite the availability of newborns as the primary reason they choose to adopt in the US. Canada and Europe don't have as many babies available for adoption. Therefore, "if you want a newborn, you go to America," says Bart van Meurs, Elisa's dad. Families also cite the health of the babies, the short waiting time, and the availability of medical records as additional advantages. Race is seldom a consideration.

"Most of our families just want a baby as young as possible, and the US is the best place to go for a newborn," explains Lorne Welwood of Hope Adoption Services in Abbotsford, British Columbia. "They are not ignoring the race issues, but they don't think, like the Americans, that the less black the better."

"The families from abroad do not think of black babies as being second best, babies that they'll 'settle' for because white babies are hard to find," says Ms. Kinnaird.

Most adoption agencies encourage the birth mother to select the adoptive family for her child. Sometimes a black birth mother prefers having her child adopted overseas because she believes there is less prejudice there than in the US.

"Some birth mothers view placing their child abroad as a way for them to have a better life with less struggle," says Joe Sica of Shepherd Care in Hollywood, Fla.

Long-term studies of black children adopted by white parents paint a picture of well-adjusted children and teens strongly bonded to their families.

Tianna Broad, who's 12, readily fits into this picture. She's into makeup, clothes, soccer, and horses, as are most of her friends in British Columbia. "She's pretty much a typical Canadian teen," says her mother, Karen Madeiros.

Most parents abroad report little prejudice against their adopted black children. "Canada doesn't have the same race history as the US," notes Dawn Stokkeland, Adrian's Elvis-rocking mom. "There isn't the 'us' versus 'them' mentality here."

There are also not the numbers of blacks in Canada. "In my son's elementary school [in British Columbia], there are only eight blacks out of 450 kids and even fewer in my daughter's middle school," says Ms. Madeiros. "Most of the blacks here are middle-class professionals, and our neighborhoods are completely integrated."

"For the most part Germans have very positive views of blacks—they see them as singers, actors, and athletes—all positive images," explains Ms. Hyer. "My children are almost always accepted for who they are without any expectation of who they should be because of the color of their skin."

"I think the main reason there is little prejudice against blacks in Germany is because there are so few blacks here," says Peter Sonnenschein, father of two black children.

That's not to say there are never problems. Some parents say their children have encountered racism.

"Because Holland had many colonies, many [black] people live here and there is prejudice against them," says van Meurs.

"Although my [12-year-old] daughter has never experienced any racism that I know of, I can't say the same for my [10-year-old] son," says Madeiros.

Parents in Canada, Germany, and the Netherlands have formed support groups to help their children develop a positive self-image.

Signs of Change

While the news may be encouraging for African-American children adopted abroad, there's evidence of change on the home front, too, as more white Americans look into adopting black babies.

Since the US doesn't keep statistics on private domestic adoptions, the exact numbers of trans-racial adoptions are not known, but anecdotal evidence abounds of a shift toward black infants being placed with white American families.

"We can find homes for all our babies in the US, but there are regional differences," notes Robert Springer of Christian Homes in Texas, who adds that "many families in the Northeast, Northwest, and Minnesota are eager to adopt African-American babies."

Dick Van Deelen, with Adoption Associates in Michigan, reports that for the first time in 35 years they have a list of white families waiting to adopt black babies.

In a twist to the import/export world of international adoption, "We are thinking of looking to Africa to bring over more children to meet this need," he says.

Adoption-Link, in Chicago, also has a waiting list of families for black babies.

"The younger generation that is now adopting is less prejudiced and more open to becoming a mixed-race family," says Mr. Van Deelen. . . .

But all the talk of adoption trends and prejudice fades in the day-to-day existence of parenting after the child arrives.

Ms. Stokkeland sums up what most parents feel. After a particularly trying day with a strong-willed 2-year-old, she sighs and says, "I wouldn't trade [Adrian] for the world. He is truly the child God wanted me to have."

The adoption was such a success that Stokkeland did it again. In October 2004, Adrian got a new little sister, as Claire Lisa, also African-American, came north from Georgia to join him and his mother in Canada. Stokkeland says she couldn't feel more blessed.

CHAPTER 3

NONTRADITIONAL ADOPTION

Gay Adoption Can Negatively Impact Children

Paul Cameron

In the following article, social psychologist Paul Cameron disputes the conclusions of the American Academy of Pediatrics (AAP) that recommended legislative efforts to allow same-sex partners to adopt children as a couple (since currently only homosexuals as individuals—not as a potential partnership—can adopt in some states). The study that provided the basis for the AAP's recommendations, Cameron argues, was deeply flawed in that it ignored the testimony of children with homosexual parents as well as clinical reports of psychiatric problems among such children. Cameron cites details from some narratives of children raised by homosexual parents, and results from research that the AAP did not consider in its study, to assert that homosexual adoption causes problems for numerous children. Cameron cites other studies that show that children raised by homosexual partners have increased chances for "acting-out behavior," self-esteem problems, and educational deficiencies. Cameron also maintains that adoption agencies should take into account yet another study that concludes that gays and lesbians have a lower median age of death than heterosexuals, thus potentially raising problems for an adopted child's future well-being. Cameron is chairman of the Family Research Institute in Colorado Springs, Colorado, and holds a doctorate in social psychology from the University of Colorado.

On Feb. 4, 2000, the American Academy of Pediatrics (AAP) recommended "legal and legislative efforts" to allow children "born to or adopted by one member of a gay or lesbian couple" to be adopted by the homosexual partner. Such a law effectively would eliminate the possibility of adoption by other family members following the death of the parent. It also would cause problems for numerous children.

The AAP, like many other professional organizations, apparently was too caught up in promoting identity politics to address all the evidence relevant to homosexual adoption. In its report, the organization offered only positive evidence about gays and lesbians as parents. "In fact," the report concluded, "growing up with parents who are lesbian or gay may confer some advantages to children." Really?

There are three sets of information on the issue: clinical reports of psychiatric disturbance of children with homosexual parents, testimonies of children with homosexual parents concerning their situation and studies that have compared the children of homosexuals with the children of nonhomosexuals. The AAP ignored the first two sets and had to cherry-pick the comparative studies to arrive at the claim that "[n]o data have pointed to any risk to children as a result of growing up in a family with one or more gay parents."

A number of clinical reports detail "acting-out behavior," homosexual seduction, elective muteness and the desire for a mother by children with homosexual parents. I am unaware of a single child being disturbed because his mother and father were married.

Sample Testimonies from Children

The AAP also ignored the testimonies of children with homosexual parents—probably the best evidence since these kids had to "live with it" rather than deal with a theory. More than 150 children with homosexual parents have provided, in extensive interviews, detailed evidence of the difficulties they encountered as a result. A study Paul and Kirk Cameron published in 2002 in *Psychological Reports* analyzed the content of 57 life-story narratives by children with homosexual parents assembled by lesbian researchers Louise Rafkin (United States) and Lisa Saffron (Britain).

In these narratives, children in 48 of the 52 families (92 percent) mentioned one or more "problems." Of the 213 problems which were scored—including hypersexuality, instability, molestation, domestic violence—children attributed 201 (94 percent) to their homosexual parent(s).

Here are four sample excerpts:

• One 9-year-old girl said: "My biological mother is S. and my other mother is L. We've lived together for a year. Before that L. lived across the street. . . . My mom met L.; L. had just broken up with someone. We moved in together because it got complicated going back and forth every night. All of a sudden I felt like I was a different person because my mom was a lesbian. . . . I get angry because I can't tell anybody about my mom. The kids at school would laugh. . . . They say awful things about lesbians . . . then they make fun of me. Having lesbian mothers is nothing to laugh about. . . . I have told my [mother] that she has made my life difficult."

• A 12-year-old boy in the United Kingdom said: "Mum . . . has had several girlfriends in my lifetime. . . . I don't go around saying that I've got two mums. . . . If we are sitting in a restaurant eating, she'll say, 'I want you to know about all these sex things.' And she'll go on about everything, just shouting it out. . . . Sometimes when mum embarrasses me, I think, 'I wish I had a dad.' . . . Been to every gay pride march. Last year, while attending, we went up to a field . . . when two men came up to us. One of them started touching me. I didn't want to go this year because of that."

• According to a 39-year-old woman: "In my memories, I'm always looking for my mother and finding her with a woman doing things I don't understand. . . . Sometimes they blame me for opening a door that wasn't even locked. . . . [At about the age of 10], I noticed a door that I hadn't yet opened. Inside I saw a big bed. My mother sat up suddenly and stared at me. She was with B. . . . and then B. shouted, 'You f***ing sneaking brat!' My mother never said a word. [Then came N.] I came to hate N. because of the way she and my mother fought every night. They screamed and bickered and whined and pouted over everything. N. closed my mother's hand in the car door. . . . She and N. hadn't made love in seven years."

• According to a 19-year-old man: "When I was about 7, my mother told me that this woman, D., was going to stay with us for a while—and she never left! I didn't think anything much about it until I was about 10. . . . It just became obvious because she and my mother were sleeping together. A few months after D. left, my mother started to see another woman, but that didn't last. Then she got involved with a different woman . . .; she'd be violent toward my mother. . . . After that she started to go on marches and to women's groups. . . . There were some women in these groups who objected to men altogether, and I couldn't cope with that."

Questionable Research Methods

The AAP ignored every comparative study of children that showed those with homosexual parents experiencing more problems. These include the largest comparative study, reported in 1996 by Sotirios Sarantakos in the journal, *Children Australia*, of 58 elementary school-children raised by coupled homosexual parents who were closely matched (by age, sex, grade in school, social class) with 58 children of cohabiting heterosexual parents and 58 raised by married parents. Teachers reported that the married couples' children scored best at math and language but somewhat lower in social studies, experienced the highest level of parental involvement at school as well as at home and had parents with the highest expectations for them. The children of homosexuals scored lowest in math and language and somewhat higher in social studies, were the least popular, experienced the lowest level of parental involvement at school and at home, had parents with the lowest expectations for them and least frequently expressed higher educational and career expectations.

Yet the AAP said that studies have "failed to document any differences between such groups on . . . academic success." The organization's report also ignored the only empirical study based upon a random sample that reported on 17 adults (out of a sample of 5,182) with homosexual parents. Detailed by Cameron and Cameron in the journal *Adolescence* in 1996, the 17 were disproportionately apt to report sexual relations with their parents, more apt to report a less than exclusively heterosexual orientation, more frequently reported gender dissatisfaction and were more apt to report that their first sexual experience was homosexual.

The AAP report also seemingly ignored a 1998 *Psychological Reports* study by Cameron and Cameron that included the largest number of children with homosexual parents. That study compared 73 children of homosexuals with 105 children of heterosexuals. Of the 66 problems cited by panels of judges who extensively reviewed the living conditions and psychological reactions of children of homosexuals undergoing a divorce from heterosexuals, 64 (97 percent) were attributed to the homosexual parent.

Finally, while ignoring studies that contradicted its own conclusions, the AAP misrepresented numerous findings from the limited literature it cited. Thus, [researcher] Sharon Huggins compared 18 children of 16 volunteer/lesbian mothers with 18 children of 16 volunteer/heterosexual/divorced mothers on self-esteem. Huggins reported statistically nonsignificant differences between the 19 children of mothers who were not living with a lover versus the 17 children of mothers who were living with a lover; and, further, that [the four] "adolescent daughters with high self-esteem had been told of their mother's lesbianism at a mean age of 6.0 years. In contrast, [the five] adolescent daughters with low self-esteem had been told at a mean age of 9.6 years" and "three of four of the mothers with high self-esteem daughters were currently living with lesbian lovers, but only one of four of the lesbian mothers with low self-esteem daughters was currently living with a lesbian lover."

The AAP cited Huggins as proving that "children's self-esteem has been shown to be higher among adolescents whose mothers (of any sexual orientation) were in a new partnered relationship after divorce, compared with those whose mother remained single, and among those who found out at a younger age that their parent was homosexual, compared with those who found out when they were older," thus transforming statistical nonevents based on niggling numbers of volunteers into important differences—twice in one sentence!

The Age of Death Factor

We have examined more than 10,000 obituaries of homosexuals: The median age of death for lesbians was in the 40s to 50s; for homosexuals it was in the 40s. Most Americans live into their 70s. Yet in the

1996 U.S. government sex survey the oldest lesbian was 49 years old and the oldest gay 54.

Children with homosexual parents are considerably more apt to lose a parent to death. Indeed, a homosexual couple in their 30s is roughly equivalent to a nonhomosexual couple in their late 40s or 50s. Adoption agencies will seldom permit a couple in their late 40s or 50s adopt a child because of the risk of parental death, and the consequent social and psychological difficulty for the child. The AAP did not address this fact—one with profound implications for any child legally related to a homosexual.

Politics Plays a Role

As usual, the media picked up on the AAP report as authoritative, assuming that it represented the consensus of a large and highly educated membership. Not so. As in other professional organizations, the vast majority of members pay their dues, read the journal and never engage in professional politics. As a consequence, a small but active minority of members gains control and uses the organization to promote its agenda. Too often, the result is ideological literature that misrepresents the true state of knowledge.

Gay-rights activists have been particularly adept at manipulating research and reports to their own ends. For years the media reported that all studies revealed that 10 percent of the population was homosexual. In fact, few if any studies ever came to that conclusion. For the next few years we will have to live with the repeated generalization that all studies prove homosexual parents are as good for children as heterosexual parents, and perhaps even better. What little literature exists on the subject proves no such thing. Indeed, translated into the language of accounting, the AAP report could be described as "cooking the books."

Gay Adoption Serves the Best Interests of Children

Shannon Minter

In the following selection, attorney Shannon Minter argues against the categorical exclusion of gays and lesbians from eligibility to adopt. While the topic of gay adoption may be a controversial political issue, Minter says, decisions on who may adopt should be made on an individual case-by-case basis, with the primary factor being the best interests of the child. Minter criticizes opponents of gay and lesbian adoption who would overlook criteria such as personality, maturity, financial stability, relationship continuity, or capacity to parent children, simply to exclude prospective parents on the basis of sexual orientation. From a child welfare perspective, Minter says, such a policy is without merit. Minter is a staff attorney for the National Center for Lesbian Rights, a legal organization based in California.

Adoption by lesbians and gay men has become a significant political issue. Especially as lesbian and gay issues have gained more visibility, . . . conservative advocates have mounted an unprecedented campaign to ban lesbians and gay men from becoming adoptive parents in a number of states. Within that highly charged political milieu, the morality of permitting lesbians and gay men to adopt is a topic of fierce and often quite vicious debate.

From a child welfare perspective, however, adoption by lesbians and gay men is a far less contentious issue. In the past, potential adoptive parents were routinely excluded from consideration on the basis of categorical factors such as age, race, religion, disability, income, and marital status. Today, state adoption laws and child welfare agencies have generally abandoned those categorical prohibitions in favor of an individualized, case-by-case assessment of the best interests of each individual child. In light of that historic shift, the great majority of legal scholars and child welfare advocates have concluded that categorical prohibitions on adoption by lesbians and gay men are harmful to children and incompatible with the best interests standard. Discrimination against lesbians and gay men in adoption has been condemned by the Child Welfare League of America (CWLA) and other professional organizations as a violation of basic principles of professional competence and responsibility. The CWLA Standards for Adoption Service Providers, which are widely accepted as the authoritative standard of care for child welfare workers, specifically provide that:

> All applicants shall be fairly assessed on their abilities to successfully parent a child needing family membership and not on their appearance, differing lifestyle, or sexual preference. (5.4). Sexual preference should not be the sole criteria on which the suitability of adoptive applicants is based. Consideration should be given to other personality and maturity factors and on the ability of the applicant to meet the specific needs of the individual child. (5.8).

Similar standards have been adopted by the American Psychological Association and the National Association of Social Workers.

In light of those professional standards, attempts to enact a categorical exclusion of lesbians and gay men from eligibility to adopt raise very serious concerns. Such a prohibition would require child welfare staff to compromise their professional and ethical responsibility to base placement decisions on generally accepted indices of children's needs and well-being. It would also force state agencies and state courts to deny adoptive placements that are in the best interests of a particular child.

The Child's Best Interests

Under current state adoption laws, the best interests of the child must be the overriding concern in any adoption proceeding. Under that standard, courts and child welfare workers are required to assess potential adoptive parents for qualities that are related to actual parenting abilities. In Utah, for example, the Utah Division of Child and Family Services (DCFS) logically evaluates the following characteristics of applicants to determine their parental fitness: ability to provide the continuity of a caring relationship; ability to provide a connection to the child's birth family if appropriate; ability to be sensitive to the child's ethnic, religious, cultural and racial heritage; and ability to understand the needs of the child at various development stages. DCFS also evaluates the prospective parent's total personality functioning; emotional maturity; quality of spousal relationship, when applicable; capacity to parent children; attitude toward childlessness and readiness to adopt; and reasons for adoption.

In contrast, a categorical ban prohibiting lesbians and gay men from eligibility to adopt would require child welfare workers and the courts to focus on sexual orientation to the exclusion of each and every one of those other relevant factors. Under such a prohibition, child welfare staff and courts would continue to evaluate the individual parenting abilities of a financially unstable heterosexual applicant with a shaky marriage and a sketchy work history, and would approve adoption by such an applicant if the adoption nonetheless was found to be in the child's best interest. At the same time, many other potentially more qualified prospective parents would be subject to automatic exclusion, including for example: a financially stable lesbian or gay man in a committed relationship with a stable work history; a lesbian or gay social worker who had an established relationship with a special needs child; and a lesbian or gay man who wished to adopt nieces, nephews or other related children whose biological parents were deceased. Those troubling outcomes graphically illustrate the irrationality of supplanting the best interest standard with generalizations that are simply not applicable in every case.

Those who advocate a ban on adoption by lesbians and gay men have not put forward any rationale that would justify sacrificing the interests of individual children in cases such as these, where placement with a lesbian or gay parent is the best option for a particular child. Notably, in fact, even Professor Lynn Wardle, who is an outspoken opponent of adoption by lesbians and gay men, has acknowledged that placement with a lesbian or gay man or with a same-sex couple may be in the best interests of an individual child.

No Evidence in Favor of Prohibition

[Since the mid-1970s], researchers who have studied children raised in a lesbian or gay parent family have found no evidence that those children are harmed or disadvantaged in any discernable way. See *American Psychological Association, Lesbian and Gay Parenting: A Resource For Psychologists* (1995) (providing annotated bibliography of empirical studies). In fact, studies have found "a remarkable absence of distinguishing features between the lifestyles, child-rearing practices, and general demographic data" of lesbian and gay parents and those who are not gay. "Not a single study has found children of gay or lesbian parents to be disadvantaged in any significant respect relative to children of heterosexual parents. Indeed, the evidence to date suggests that home environments provided by gay and lesbian parents are as likely as those provided by heterosexual parents to support and enable children's psychosocial growth."

Some opponents of adoption by lesbians and gay men have sought to justify their position on the ground that the entire body of social science research on children of lesbian and gay parents is methodologically flawed. For many years, the primary spokesperson for that view was Dr. Paul Cameron, who has been reprimanded by both the courts and the general scientific community for misrepresenting research on lesbian and gay people. More recently, a similarly critical view of social science research on lesbian and gay parents has been put forward by Professor Lynn Wardle, who relies on Dr. Cameron, among others, in attempting to substantiate his critique. Although considerations of space preclude a detailed response to those views here, a few key points deserve specific mention.

Professor Wardle's primary contention is that studies of lesbian and gay parent families lack "external validity" because "not a single study remotely represented any sub-population of homosexual parents." In fact, more than 40 studies of lesbian and gay parents have been undertaken, including parents from a wide range of geographic areas and a mix of urban and non-urban environments. None of those studies has produced evidence that lesbian and gay parents are harmful to children, or that sexual orientation is relevant to parental ability. It is the accumulation of consistent results from many different sample groups, not the results of any one specific study, that has established a meaning body of data. As in many other research areas, the absence of any way to identify the entire population (in this case, of lesbian and gay parents) does not preclude meaningful research or invalidate the significant body of research that already exists. Thus, while the limitations of various individual studies have been noted, both by the researchers themselves and by others, the overall significance and validity of those repeated findings has not been subject to any significant academic dispute.

Professor Wardle also maintains that studies on lesbian and gay parents are meaningless because they do not control for "income, education, employment, health, extended family and other support systems, age, religion, support programs, siblings, and other factors." In fact, however, many of the studies control for the very factors that he cites.

In addition, if applied as a general rule, this concern would invalidate the great majority of all studies on parenting. By its very nature, research on a subject as complex and multi-faceted as parenting cannot possibly control for every conceivable "variable that may influence the success of parenting or the well-being of children." One of the most important goals of research on children is to identify the variables that are relevant to good parenting, and it is the overwhelming conclusion of all the research that exists to date that the sexual orientation of a parent is not a particularly relevant concern.

In sum, while researchers in this area have readily acknowledged the limitations of various individual studies, the body of research on lesbian and gay parents is well within the boundaries of legitimate academic research. It provides a strong empirical basis for the proposition that there is no basis for any generalized concerns about the well-being of children raised by lesbian and gay parents. As many scholars have stressed, the research on lesbian and gay parents does not purport to show that all lesbians and gay men are by definition good parents, any more than research shows that all heterosexual people or all married people are by definition good parents. What the research does show, however, is that there is nothing inherent to being a lesbian or gay man that precludes a person from being a good parent, and thus no reason for lesbians and gay men to be subject to special rules or exclusions as potential adoptive parents.

A Child Welfare Perspective

Attempts to exclude all lesbian and gay people from the pool of potential adoptive parents have little merit from a child welfare perspective. When confronted with arguments that purport to support such a categorical ban, child welfare advocates should scrutinize those arguments carefully. Although political debates about adoption by lesbians and gay men are almost certain to rage on, child welfare policies should be driven by and accountable to the welfare of each and every child in state custody, not by partisan ideologies that are at odds with accepted child protection standards. Under those standards, there is no legitimate reason to exclude lesbians and gay men as potential adoptive parents, or to prohibit a court from approving adoption petitions by a lesbian or a gay man when it is in the best interests of an individual child.

TRANSRACIAL ADOPTION

Samiya A. Bashir

The practice of placing black children in white adoptive families has increased in the last thirty years, Samiya A. Bashir notes in the following article, and so has the controversy it generates. Bashir quotes proponents of transracial adoption who argue that removing racial barriers will reduce the disproportionately large number of black children awaiting placement in foster care. Bashir also cites black social workers and adoption agencies who say that same-race placements are better for a child's racial identity and better prepare black children for life in a racist society. These latter advocates say that there should be a greater emphasis placed on recruitment of black adoptive families, not on the creation of multiracial adoptive families. Bashir is a writer and coeditor of *Role Call: A Generational Anthology of Social & Political Black Literature & Art*.

In a landmark 1972 statement, the National Association of Black Social Workers (NABSW) declared its opposition to transracial adoption. It called the practice of placing black children in white adoptive families "a blatant form of racial and cultural genocide." The NABSW cited, as reasons for their position, concerns that the practice isolated children from their racial and cultural identity, and would leave them unprepared to live in a racist society.

The NABSW's controversial statement, and the supporting position paper it released, was just the tip of a now long-running debate, carried out in the "best interests" of children too young to articulate the situation for themselves. The struggle to communicate about the subject was not limited to the adoptees. Everyone involved—children, adoptive parents, birthparents, and adoption professionals—was wading in uncharted waters with only the most limited language available to articulate the issues.

The NABSW took its position just five years after the 1967 Supreme Court case, *Loving v. Virginia*, which annulled state laws against interracial marriages. A generation earlier, the idea of white parents wanting to adopt black children would have seemed almost unthinkable.

But, between 1968 and 1972, approximately 50,000 black and biracial children were adopted into white families. The changing racial climate and shifting attitudes toward adoption combined with other factors such as the limited number of healthy, available white infants, to bring the unthinkable to the center of national debate.

[Since 1992], transracial adoptions have counted for about 15 percent of U.S. adoptions. As the first sizable generation of transracial adoptees, born in the mid-60s to mid-70s, come of age, their experiences are finally being added to the debate which has long been waged without them.

Catherine McKinley explores her own experiences in her memoir *The Book of Sarahs*. McKinley, a biracial woman whose birth mother is Jewish and birth father is African American, was adopted by a white family in rural Massachusetts. "We don't have the voices of a lot of transracial adoptees," said McKinley. "There is a huge sea of stories that need to be out there."

Still, many adoptees find it difficult to have their voices heard. "They're all looking for this 'authentic voice,'" said McKinley. "If you don't offer the same predictable ideas about transracial adoption then people become really uncomfortable."

Waiting for Families

Proponents of transracial adoption argue that because black children are more likely to be in foster care than white children, stay in foster care longer, and are more likely to undergo multiple placements, opening the process to adoption across color lines is the answer to the problems of both children and would-be parents.

In Massachusetts, where McKinley was raised, only 5 percent of the population is African American. Yet, African American children represent almost 50 percent of children awaiting placement. Nationwide, 40 percent of children awaiting adoption are black. In urban areas, like New York City, those numbers climb to 75 percent. The average wait for a child in foster care to be placed is almost three years. For African American children, the wait can stretch to twice the average.

Many proponents of transracial adoption argue that there are not enough families of color who wish to adopt. In fact, it has been shown that black families foster and adopt children, often under informal arrangements, at a far higher rate than the general population. A 1977 study published by the National Urban League concluded that 90 percent of African American children born out of wedlock are informally adopted. A subsequent study, sponsored in 1984 by the U.S. Department of Health and Human Services, showed that African American families adopt 4.5 times more than any other ethnic group.

Instead, the NABSW, along with a number of black adoption agencies, argue that families of color are routinely passed over in favor of white families. They claim that child welfare agencies, staffed primarily with white social workers, have long turned a blind eye to systems which stand in the way of joining prospective parents of color with children in need.

The North American Council on Adoptable Children's 1991 study, "Barriers to Same Race Placement," found that African American–run adoption agencies successfully placed 94 percent of black children with black families. Organizations like the Association of Black Social Workers' Child Adoption, Detroit's Homes for Black Children, the nationwide One Church, One Child Program, and Los Angeles's Institute for Black Parents all show successful intraracial placements.

The Black Pulse Survey, conducted between 1981 and 1993 and published by the National Urban League, found three million African American households interested in adoption. The study's numbers suggested that, were even a tiny fraction of those families allowed to adopt, any argument about a preponderance of children in search of loving black homes would be effectively moot.

Rooted in Inequality

The NABSW has claimed that its resolution, and the position paper that followed, was directed not at children or parents. Instead, it sought to redirect the discussion about transracial adoption to identify how seemingly race-neutral policies were actually carried out by a system entrenched in racially motivated decisions and practices.

Transracial adoption must be considered within the larger discussion of the impoverishment and annihilation of black families and communities, the NABSW argued, along with numerous community groups. The group claimed that child welfare workers have historically made relatively few retention efforts with African American birth parents and extended families. Black families who attempt to adopt through traditional means are often met with discrimination or discouragement. They further argue that fewer efforts are made to reunite African American foster children with their families of origin.

Significant institutional barriers exist, such as the bureaucratic systems that control the licensing and recruitment of foster and adoptive families, which often prevent or discourage families of color from applying to adopt. African American families who do apply are frequently screened out of the process due to racist attitudes, economic barriers, and a widespread lack of cultural understanding which frequently categorizes difference as pathology. Families of color are often markedly different from the normative, Eurocentric model and include greater involvement of extended families, more family members living together, and a wider division of childcare.

Foster care has become a billion-dollar business in which agencies receive between $15,000 and $100,000 per child, per year in government funds. The financial incentive for public agencies to recruit and retain children—lest they be out of business—is met by an equally discouraging financial burden placed on parents by private agencies.

Prospective parents can expect to pay between $5,000 and $50,000 to a private agency to adopt. Blacks are the "least expensive" children available, which, combined with a historical aversion to the buying and selling of African American children, often serves as a psychological barrier for black families seeking service. Consequently, 50 percent of black children placed by private agencies are adopted transracially.

Racial Politics in the Home

Few argue the destructive effects of leaving children to languish in the fractured foster care system. However, there is no agreement that transracial adoption is the way out.

One fact that seldom reaches the debate is that 44 percent of children available for adoption nationwide are white children. However, most of those children are school-aged or have special needs. The greatest demand among all races is for the infants and toddlers who make up only 4 percent of all adoptable children. Some argue that the debate over transracial adoption is accordingly more concerned with the rights of whites to have access to adoptable infants than the rights of children to placement in loving and appropriate homes.

In a recent study, Amanda L. Baden, Ph.D., of St. John's University, argues that transracial adoptees' exposure and competence in their birth culture may not be necessary for good psychological adjustment. The study, which was conducted through survey questionnaires with adult (ages 19–36) African American and Latina/o transracial adoptees, asserts that those who identified strongly with white culture fared no worse than those who identified with their birth culture.

The methodology behind Baden's study, which had no control group of intraracially adopted children, has been widely criticized by opponents and adoptees. However, so few studies of adult adoptees exist that her work is often offered as a credible resource in the defense of the practice. This is where the voices of the adoptees themselves become even more essential.

Jasper Steenhuis, a biracial man who was adopted into a large, multiracial family, was raised with "a large adoptive families' community," which he said fed him as he grew up.

But McKinley felt resentful of being forced to socialize with other transracial adoptees as a child. "I felt terribly outside of everything and everybody," she said. "Truthfully my parents didn't tell me very much. My [white] brother often wasn't even referred to as adopted, and even when he was an 'adopted child,' I was a 'transracial adoptee.'"

McKinley insisted that having racial models throughout childhood and adolescence are crucial. "How do you find out where the line is between the black female experience and the transracial adoption experience?" she asked. "I have friends who grew up with black parents who had the same experiences. When I was little I needed a community where people could say, 'Girl, this is normal!'"

Baden asserts that "transracial adoptees who function adequately in the white culture, and who do not reject white culture, may report less psychological distress. If this relationship is shown to exist, it could suggest that psychological adjustment would naturally be poorer for those transracial adoptees who did not accept, or at least function well within, the culture of their parents."

For some this smacks of the very cultural genocide the NABSW warned against. "I don't believe that whole assimilation model," said McKinley. "I think people can pretend or buy into it to a particular degree, but I don't think it's true."

Still, McKinley pointed out that family is not necessarily the sole arbiter of racial identity. "There's a myth that you get your identity from your parents," she said. "It's a combination of so many things. I'm as black socialized as any of my peers, and I didn't get it at home. I think home sets an environment that makes you go out and search for things from the outside."

Steenhuis, whose adoptive parents are Dutch immigrants, faced compound hurdles on the road to racial identity, but he also had a great deal more peer support. The Steenhuises, a nursery school teacher and a university professor, had one biological child, and adopted eight more of different races. Two of his sisters are biologically related, Native and African American girls who were adopted together. One adoptee is white, and the others are various mixes of African American, Native American, and Jewish.

Although the family lived in a small, predominately white college town, his parents remained vigilant about providing role models of color to their children. "It may have seemed like a token gesture to make sure there was an *Ebony* subscription at my house," laughed Steenhuis, "but it did matter."

The Steenhuises were actively involved in transracial adoptive support groups and family organizations. The kids were also enrolled in a predominately black after-school program to counter their largely white school environments.

By high school, Jasper was involved in sports. He joined a track team, where he ran with a number of other African American kids. But his isolation from a diverse, neighborhood peer group still had its effect. "I'd wake up in the morning and hang out with the white kid across the street," said Steenhuis. To his African American friends across town, "I was a good friend, but we didn't grow up together, and that means something."

"My racial identity really became a big thing once I got to college," continued Steenhuis, "because you start over. Freshman and sophomore years were a whole new world. I went a little overboard," he added with a chuckle. "I probably didn't have to run for the Black Student Union presidency."

Supporting Transracial Adoptive Families

In 1994, the NABSW softened their position by saying that transracial adoption may be considered, but only after "documented evidence of unsuccessful same-race placements have been reviewed and supported by appropriate representatives of the African American community."

"You do have to put priority on matching people up with families that are of the same race," said Steenhuis. "The first priority is finding good parents, and then I think race should be an issue. It is more difficult, but effort counts in life. Parenting isn't easy, and no matter what child you raise it's going to be difficult."

Most agree that in the interim, the families that exist need to be supported. "I don't see any evidence that transracial adoption is going to stop," said Judith Ashton, a white adoptive parent and executive director of the New York Citizens Coalition for Children. "The best thing we can do is see that parents get the skills they need so they can do a better job."

"Parents are more accepting today of the fact that they cannot protect their child from the reality of racism," she added, "and that their task is not to protect but to prepare. It's evidence of another kind of racism, that sense of white privilege, that nobody made demands of us—nobody ever asked us what we had to bring to this child that was going to help develop a positive self-identity in a racist society."

As adoptees become more vocal, adding their realities to the mountains of speculation, it may well be their experiences—more than the opinions of policy wonks, or even the parents themselves—that determine the future of the next generation of children in search of a loving home.

"Adoption is the best situation you can make out of a bad situation," said Steenhuis. "I had a great experience, but I can't tell you everybody did. There are definitely families where it didn't go well at all. Some of that is the baggage kids bring and some of it is because the parents were not really aware that: 'Hey, these kids are black folks, and their race does matter.'"

ADOPTING A TEENAGER

Amy Engeler

Adopting a teenager presents unique challenges, as reporter Amy Engeler describes in the following selection. Engeler states that children over the age of nine are unlikely to be adopted because they are entering an age when they are more likely to push boundaries and "test" parents with their behavior, and potential adoptive parents become wary of the emotional baggage carried by children who have spent years in foster care or group homes. Citing examples of parents who adopted teenagers, Engeler concludes that adoptions of older children are more likely to be successful if adoptive parents have had some exposure to the adoptee—as a tutor, mentor, or social worker—before the adoption is officially undertaken. Engeler is a freelance writer and reporter.

Leora Hartman, a longtime Lakewood, Colorado, real estate broker, will never forget her first glimpse of Sonya, the child she brought into her life seven years ago. Eleven at the time, the girl was thin with straw-colored hair, and wore brown lipstick and gobs of mascara. A pair of sandals exposed her bare feet and legs to the bitter winter wind, a tight shirt pulled at her breasts, and the filling in her shabby down coat had settled around her wrists.

Sonya lived with her alcoholic mother at various cheap motels and had been in minor trouble with the law for bringing a marijuana pipe to her fourth-grade classroom. Leora, a volunteer with the Jefferson County Children's Advocacy Center, had been assigned to drive the child from school to court-ordered therapy once a week and to help her with a research paper (also court-ordered) on the effects of marijuana.

Sonya hopped into Leora's car in her nonchalant way, as though nothing were amiss. But over the next few months, Leora could sense the need under Sonya's bravely cool facade. Although Sonya rarely complained or asked for anything, Leora felt the child trying to stretch out their time together; the research paper eventually turned into a 40-page epic.

Leora was divorced with two grown children and hadn't meant to become so involved in the girl's life. One June evening, as she returned with Sonya to the motel after a shopping trip, she opened the door and found Sonya's mother in bed with a man. "I heard Sonya say, 'Oh, did I come at a bad time?'" Leora remembers. "It broke my heart. It was so matter of fact, this not-yet-12-year-old girl talking to her mother that way."

Leora brought the girl home and set her up in the guest bedroom for the night. The next day, when they returned to the motel, a man was lounging in the room; there was no sign of Sonya's mother. Seeing the girl cower, Leora knew she had no choice but to pack Sonya back into the car, this time for good.

Leora called the advocacy center and reported that Sonya was in danger—already physically mature, the child was living in unsafe conditions without supervision. Then the 52-year-old Leora took Sonya in as a foster child. Three years later, after the child's mother and father (who did not live with them) relinquished parental rights, Leora adopted Sonya. "Why this kid?" a social worker asked. "Because this kid has absolutely no one," Leora answered. "It was as simple as that."

Older Children, Longer Odds

Few people would dream of taking in a hormone-laden, boundary-pushing, and, at times, mercurial adolescent. When it comes to adoption, most parents still want an infant. Although the picture is brightening for adolescents like Sonya—she was one of nearly 10,000 older children adopted from foster care in the year 2000, a 54 percent increase from just two years earlier—far too many still languish in transient foster homes.

Out of sheer necessity—and in response to kids' requests—the social services community is finally turning its attention to getting these older kids hooked up with permanent families. To help, President [George W.] Bush is urging Congress to reward states for placing older children and teenagers in adoptive homes.

Once a child passes the age of nine in foster care, the odds are against adoption. Potential parents are wary, concerned about the emotional baggage a kid carries from a life of isolation. The best way to get around these fears, say caseworkers, is to wait for a relationship to develop between the child and a trusted adult—a tutor, mentor, social worker, basketball coach, or manager at the local burger franchise—before the idea of adoption is raised.

That's what happened to Dave Brown, a pilot, after the United Way paired him as a mentor with Chris, a shy, depressed 13-year-old orphan living in a children's home in California, Kentucky. The two hit it off so well, Dave himself proposed the adoption, becoming a single father at age 37.

Kim Stevens and her husband, Buddy, went to an adoption party—an event set up by social workers for prospective parents to meet kids in a relaxed atmosphere—hoping to find a little girl between the ages of their two biological sons, two and eight. But once they'd spent the afternoon playing with 15-year-old Jim, they were hooked. "It was clear from the moment we met him that he belonged in our family," Kim says now. "This sounds hokey, but we felt we 'recognized' him. It was the same feeling we had when our babies were born."

From Foster Care to Families

For a long time, professional wisdom had it that teenagers were too old to bond with a new family and would be better off living in a group residence with their peers. And yet, some advocates, like Pat O'Brien of the Brooklyn-based adoption agency You Gotta Believe, have argued for years that getting teenagers into permanent families is not only humane but beneficial for society. Studies from the mid-1990s show that the 20,000 or so young adults who age out of the foster care system each year go into the world with little more than pocket change and are very likely to end up homeless, on welfare, or in prison. Fewer than half earn their high school diploma, and only a small fraction become self-sufficient by their 20s. Hardly surprising, says O'Brien. "These days you have kids who grew up in intact, two-parent homes still living with their folks at 28 or 29 years old," he notes. "How can you expect an 18-year-old to do better after growing up in foster care?"

O'Brien produces a weekly public access television program, *Adopting Teens & 'Tweens*. In one installment filmed in the fall of 2002 in a church meeting room, he assembled three youngsters seeking adoptive parents. Looking at the kids, you might see some attitude, but you also sense profound loneliness. "Why do you want to be adopted?" O'Brien asked the group. "Someone to be there," one boy stammered, then looked shyly down at the floor.

Paul Snellgrove saw some of this sadness in Keith, a sensitive, well-behaved 13-year-old he had known for years through his job as a social worker. It was always assumed that Keith's "quasi-grandmother" would adopt him once his substance-abusing mother ran out of chances. But she refused to take him in when the time came, leaving Keith without much chance of finding a permanent family.

"My heart goes out to this kid," Paul told his wife, Margaret Roman, one afternoon in 1990. Both had recently turned 40, and they had just about given up on fertility treatments. "You want our first child to be a teenager?" Margaret replied, incredulous. "I want to adopt a child, but not a teenager."

Paul calmly asked if she'd like to see a picture of the boy. "No, I don't want to see a picture," she answered. He left one anyway, on the shelf where Margaret kept her house keys. Over the next few weeks, her attitude softened. She went to parenting classes with Paul, who told her more and more about the boy. "I was sucked in," she says. "Once somebody creeps into your heart, that decides it. He was adorable."

Keith himself remembers feeling "overwhelmed" when he learned that Paul and Margaret were going to adopt him. He arrived at the couple's Rockaway, New Jersey, house as a seventh grader, which meant they didn't have to worry about things like baby-sitters or day care. Yet when Margaret came home from her job as a college English professor, Keith would play the same type of bonding games as toddlers do, looking for the same kind of reassurance. Although he was only six inches shorter than Margaret, Keith liked to stand on the tops of her feet and be walked around like a puppet. He also hid when he heard her coming up the long steps to their house, which is perched on the top of a hill at the edge of a forest preserve. "I'd have to call 'Where's Keith?' and search all around for him," Margaret says. "It scared me half to death if I couldn't find him right away."

Testing Times

For the first few years, Keith struggled at school—mostly from lack of interest. At home, though, he was fun and open. The family has numerous photographs that show him smiling broadly, as he grew taller and leaner. Then, almost exactly three years later, when Margaret and Paul finalized plans to adopt an 11-year-old girl, Keith's honeymoon (as researchers call the carefree early period of teenage adoptions) suddenly ended. A period of testing set in. Keith was cursing at his parents, stealing from them—and he was doing drugs. Paul was so angry, he didn't even want to look at his son.

Now a handsome, responsible 26-year-old with a job at a large pharmaceutical company, Keith understands exactly what was going on. "In the beginning, I tried to fit in. Once I knew that this place was really mine, I did stupid things that I wasn't supposed to do within the family, and I also did things that any teenager would." Why? he's asked. "I was testing them, to see if they really wanted me."

Researchers at the University of South Carolina's Center for Child and Family Studies have found some degree of testing in virtually every adoption they've documented. "A number of these kids told me that they were really terrible to their parents, even though they loved them," says Cynthia Flynn, the lead researcher for the study.

The Snellgroves tried therapy, but while Keith went willingly enough, he wouldn't open up with the counselor. Thinking about his birth mother and her failure with him was "hard to take," he admits now. Keith's behavior caused friction between Paul and Margaret, as Paul found it difficult to control his feelings of fury and Margaret tried to defend their son. "I knew how to tick off my dad," Keith acknowledges now. "But my mom was always there, no matter what I did."

Margaret and Paul did find help at a local support group for similarly anguished parents. And they got some satisfaction from the realization that every other mother and father in the room had a kid in just as much trouble as Keith—and those were their biological children.

Living with Family Ghosts

After her removal from her mother's motel-room home, Sonya spent the summer in protective custody, then moved into Leora Hartman's comfortable house in time to start sixth grade. Leora's own son and daughter were supportive of their mother's decision, but she lost a few friends, people who couldn't understand why she would want to take in this wayward child.

Almost immediately, Sonya dropped her tough facade, stopped drinking and smoking pot, put away the makeup, and kept to a scheduled day. The stability felt "a little weird," she says now. Sonya also had to learn to be a child again. "Because she'd parented her mother for so long, she was used to being the grown-up," Leora recalls, "and would say odd things like 'Isn't it time for us to go to bed?'"

Leora turned all her energy to helping Sonya, who attended five sessions of therapy a week. Food issues surfaced; in a house with a well-stocked refrigerator, Sonya first gorged herself, then grew weight-conscious and very thin. An epileptic, she became something of a hypochondriac, too, Leora says.

It was like parenting in double time, cramming ten years of guidance into the first one with the teen. "Leora was amazing," says Sonya, now 18. When Sonya misbehaved, Leora would send her to her room to write a letter explaining why she had done it. "That was the best punishment for me," says Sonya, "because I had to think about my behavior, and therefore, I could improve it."

Part of Two Families

Meanwhile, Sonya began to take violin and riding lessons, eventually winning a spot on a precision horse team that performs at stock and rodeo shows. Perhaps not surprisingly, the girl's comfortable new life (supported by Leora's real estate business and a $400-per-month state subsidy) aroused envy in members of Sonya's biological family. Leora, they felt, was meddling "in their business."

Helping Sonya bridge these two worlds became Leora's biggest challenge. But it's a necessary one for adoptive parents of teenagers, according to experts. Many successful adoptions, says Cynthia Flynn, keep the connections to the child's past, even if they are disruptive.

As the date of Sonya's formal adoption drew near, she began to struggle academically, distracted by her relatives' disapproval. "I was told I wasn't going to be part of the family anymore, that Leora was dumb and shouldn't have stuck her nose in," says Sonya. The guilt, she remembers, "was overwhelming."

With Leora's support, Sonya made it through the worst, realizing that even if she had a new mother, these people would always be her relatives. Once the adoption became final, she became more at peace. "I tell my friends I used to do drugs," says Sonya, who is starting as a biology major at the University of Northern Colorado. . . . "They are like, 'You? The teacher's pet?'"

Sonya knows how far she's come. "It was pretty crazy," she says. "I definitely wouldn't be here without Leora. She grabbed hold of me—and I grabbed on for dear life."

No Guaranteed Successes

Some teens aren't as lucky: As many as 15 percent of adoptions involving older and special-needs children fail, according to the National Adoption Center. Dee Weaver, 19, of Charlotte, North Carolina, survived one unhappy adoption experience. Her adoptive mother seemed "nice and sympathetic," but once Dee moved in, the woman turned verbally hostile, telling the 13-year-old that her hair was ugly, that she was fat and lazy, and that she smelled. After nine months, Dee begged her social workers to send her back to a group residence.

"We try to turn families upside down in terms of screening," says Ruth Amerson, director of Another Choice, the adoption agency that placed Dee. "But sometimes we're wrong." The woman who adopted Dee had wanted to rescue a kid from the system, to give back to the community, Amerson explains. But occasionally, "there is a difference between what people want to do and what they can do."

Amerson pleaded with Mike and Wanda Weaver to take the child for a short time, until a space opened up at Dee's former group home. The Weavers, who'd just adopted a six-year-old boy through Amerson's agency, weren't sure. They worried that Dee might be too old and too rebellious to accept their love and guidance, but they reluctantly agreed.

Like many kids who have spent most of their lives in foster care—Dee had been in from age six—she seemed young for her age. She was also depressed, according to the Weavers, her head hanging so low that she had developed a hump on the back of her neck. The beginning didn't go well. Dee put her suitcase down in the bedroom she was going to share with the Weavers' 11-year-old biological daughter, Audrey, and refused to unpack. "Why bother?" she muttered, avoiding eye contact. "I'll be moving on soon."

The Power of Love

At first, the Weavers respected her distance. But, Dee explains today, as much as she told herself not to grow attached to these people and possibly be hurt again, she felt herself being drawn into the family. First she opened up to Audrey, who seemed to love having an older sister. Mike and Wanda could hear the girls talking late into the night. Then Dee became close to boisterous Mike, who told her all about his own grief at losing his mother, father, and brother.

Gradually, she began to feel connected with Wanda, who performed a very deft makeover on Dee, taking her to hair salons and clothing stores. And Dee liked coming home from school to tell the couple about her day. "They were young and understood what it was like to be a teenager," she says.

A few weeks turned into a few months, then a year. With the agency's approval, Mike told Dee that he and Wanda considered her a permanent member of the family and if she wished, they'd go through the paperwork to make it legal.

Dee mulled it over for weeks. Finally, she took that brave step and agreed to another adoption.

Experts caution that teenagers who are "rescued" from foster care may not always be able to show gratitude or express affection, but adoptive parents say the satisfaction that comes from making a difference in a young person's life can be enormous. Mike insists he's gotten more out of the experience than Dee herself. "She has made me a better person," he says.

Dee is now a sophomore in college, with a steady boyfriend, a relationship she would not have been able to manage, she says, had she stayed in foster care. "Mike and Wanda didn't have to do what they did, but they have so much love and kindness in their hearts, they took me in," she says. "I don't think they realize how much I owe them."

CHAPTER 4

OPENNESS AND DISCLOSURE

THE BENEFITS OF OPEN ADOPTION

Adam Pertman

In the following selection, author Adam Pertman presents the benefits of open adoption—adoptions in which adopted children and their new parents remain in contact with the birth parents. Pertman notes that open adoptions are becoming more common and that expanding openness is the "central characteristic of the adoption revolution." Pertman argues that open adoption arrangements provide adoptees with a sense of self-knowledge and identity. He also states that openness allows birth parents to be more comfortable with the idea of giving up a child, and it affords adoptive parents maximum background information about their adopted children. Pertman was a senior reporter and editor for the *Boston Globe* for twenty-two years. He is now executive director of the Evan B. Donaldson Adoption Institute.

No one had coerced or pressured or embarrassed Donna into relinquishing her baby for adoption. She was motivated by the same core concern that leads nearly all women, and men when they are involved, to make this excruciating decision today. While they know that physiologically they can become mothers and fathers, they strongly believe they aren't prepared to be parents. The distinction may sound subtle, but it's critical.

Most often, these are women in their late teens to mid-twenties who lack the financial or personal resources to raise a child, or whose lives would be turned inside-out if they tried. Or they suffer from problems they don't want to inflict on a child. Sometimes they're rape victims who can't face the prospect of rearing their attackers' offspring. Increasingly, they're couples who already have one or more children but feel their families would be impossibly strained if they had another mouth to feed. And they are often well-educated. Researchers say women who are younger, or have less schooling, tend to think less about the consequences of their decisions, and therefore are more prone to keep their babies.

Two threads bind these varied participants at the genesis of domestic infant adoption: They do not opt for abortion, even though it of-

Adam Pertman, *Adoption Nation: How the Adoption Revolution Is Transforming America.* New York: Basic Books, 2000. Copyright © 2000 by Adam Pertman. All rights reserved. Reproduced by permission of Basic Books, a member of Perseus Books LLC.

ten carries less social stigma for biological parents than does placing their children in new homes; and they want good lives for their babies, better than they believe they can provide. The lingering cultural stereotype of birth mothers as uncaring or ignorant young teens who choose adoption to crassly jettison a nettlesome problem is unmitigated and corrosive nonsense.

Donna's Story

Donna was lying on a surgical table at an abortion clinic in 1986 when she realized that adoption was the only alternative she could live with. She could barely believe she had walked into this place to begin with; just a few years earlier, after all, she had been president of a Right to Life chapter at her high school. "I was on my back there for what seemed like the longest time, talking to God out loud, asking him, 'What am I doing here?'" she recalls. When the doctor finally approached her, Donna bolted upright and raised her voice: "You will not touch me!"

Donna had fallen in love with "Mr. Wonderful" while she was a 20-year-old junior at the University of Kentucky. Two months later she was pregnant, he was gone, and her sister persuaded her to temporarily move in with her in Nashville, so she would have some support while considering what to do. After she left the abortion clinic, Donna began a process identical to the one many women follow in comparable situations. She opened the Yellow Pages and looked under "attorneys" and "adoption." She was drawn, in the latter category, to a phone number for the local Catholic Charities adoption agency.

In the months that followed, Donna received counseling, read letters, and looked at photos from an array of prospective parents, and was repeatedly given the opportunity to change her mind. She offers only praise for the procedure that preceded her giving birth, but nothing could have prepared her for the emotions that seized her at the end. No matter how sure pregnant women believe they are about parting with their babies, regardless of what impact they think their decisions might have, irrespective of what might seem right or wrong, at least half change their minds once they feel their babies emerging, or hold them, or nurse them or are confronted with the impossible task of forever handing them over to virtual strangers.

The point of sharpest impact for Donna came after she had carried her daughter out of the hospital, which she insisted on doing, and after her counselor had strapped the three-day-old girl into a carrier in the back seat of her Jeep. Donna is a true believer in adoption. For years now, she has worked as a pregnancy and adoption counselor herself for the agency that once helped her. She insists she has no regrets about what she did. But Donna doesn't try to fool herself about the emotions she experienced as she watched the car drive away that day. "It was the most painful moment of my entire life," she says.

The Birth Mother Plays a Role

During the years that followed, Donna resumed her studies and plowed ahead. She fell in love with her husband-to-be, and they had a baby daughter in 1998. Donna says her healing process, especially early on, was helped considerably by the pictures and letters she regularly received from Kelly's adoptive parents, Carol and Michael Wierzba. Knowing the girl was happy and loved reinforced Donna's feeling that she had done the right thing. Occasionally she daydreamed about seeing Kelly again, but she didn't want to interfere with her upbringing and figured it would be too complicated until the Wierzbas' daughter (as she now thought of her) was much older. So Donna was flabbergasted when, out of nowhere, an employee from the adoption agency called to say that Michael and Carol wanted to take her out to dinner. Kelly was 18 months old, and the Wierzbas wanted to explore the possibility of her birth mother occupying a larger place in her life.

"At first, I told them thanks, but I don't think so. I mean, I just couldn't imagine what they were thinking. I didn't know if I could handle it. I didn't know if Kelly could handle it. The truth is I didn't know what to think, I was so in shock." Donna laughs at the memory. She says it quickly dawned on her that she had nothing to lose in just talking to the Wierzbas, though she feared she'd be so nervous she wouldn't give a good impression. Her voice quivering, she told the agency worker, "Tell them that I said okay." They set a date and a time and hung up. "Only then did I realize what was happening and what was possible. I was bouncing off the walls. All I could think was what a lucky person I am."

And unusual. Arrangements like the one the Wierzbas now share with Donna, in which she is a constant in her daughter's life, are still the exception. They are growing less rare by the day, however, and some degree of regular contact between biological and adoptive families is rapidly becoming commonplace by letter, on the phone, or in person. The main reasons are simple to understand, because they promote honesty and respect, yet difficult to internalize, because they can cause uneasiness and demand selflessness.

Benefits for Adoptees and Birth Mothers

First and foremost, social-work and mental-health experts have reached a consensus during the last decade that greater openness offers an array of benefits for adoptees—from ongoing information about family medical issues to fulfillment of their innate desire to know about their genetic histories—even if the expanded relationships themselves prove difficult or uncomfortable for some of the participants.

At the same time, adoption professionals have learned that they lived in a fantasy world for generations and are coming to terms with a hard truth about birth mothers: The vast majority do not "forget and get on with their lives," as though they were machines built to incubate life and give it away. In fact, most of these women sustain emotional and psychic injuries, no matter how good they consider their reasons or how much denial they permit themselves. Overwhelmingly, later in life if not right away, whether they say so out loud or only whisper the truth to themselves in the protective darkness of sleepless nights, they yearn for contact with or knowledge about their children.

Adoption is supposed to help people, not torment them. So, as the consequences of the old ways have become clear, adoption agencies and attorneys who arrange "closed" adoptions have become an endangered species. It's a remarkable reversal from the standard operating procedure of past decades, when all identifying data about birth and adoptive parents were guarded like nuclear secrets—and the very idea of a face-to-face meeting was considered perverse. "What's wrong with her? Why can't she just get on with her life?" social workers asked if a birth mother hinted she'd like to know how her baby was doing. Adoptees and adoptive parents were viewed as ungrateful, perhaps even unstable, if they sought information about the people who made their families possible.

Some birth parents still seek confidentiality, and a small percentage presumably always will because of their personalities or circumstances. But as society and the adoption system permit them to feel less guilt and shame about their decisions, the ranks of the anonymous are dwindling. Most often now, it's the adoptive mothers and fathers who are apprehensive about openness—though, again, in smaller and smaller numbers.

Adoptive Parents Overcome Concerns

Caution and protectiveness are understandable emotions for anyone with normal instincts and insecurities, but all the more so for most adoptive parents. Our sensitivities about raising a family usually have been heightened by fertility problems that prevented us from producing biological children, then our self-confidence has been further shaken by the emotionally turbulent voyage that adoption invariably entails. As hard as it may be to accept, however, the adoptive parents' gut-level concerns about the consequences of openness are usually exaggerated and often unfounded.

Most reassuring is the fact that there's no clinical or practical evidence to indicate adoptees or birth parents try to disrupt or interfere with adoptions that include sustained contact. To the contrary, many adoptions grow stronger and all three members of the triad become more secure when their relationships cease to be based on fear and fantasy.

In the vast majority of cases, anyway, it's the adoptive parents who are the gatekeepers and decide the extent and timing of any participation (or even knowledge) by their children. While adoptees generally are curious, and ask more and more questions as they get older, they typically don't request detailed information or consider the possibility of in-person meetings until they are into their teens. It's also unusual for adoptees to seek out their biological parents before they are well into their twenties or thirties, ordinarily as planning for their own futures heightens their desire to know more about their pasts.

That's the current, fading snapshot. But, like everything else about adoption, the new picture still hasn't come into focus. Every day, more and more adoptive mothers and fathers are making contact with birth parents while their children are still very small. Adoptees are exploring their roots at younger and younger ages, empowered in part by the extraordinary resources of the Internet, while birth mothers, fathers, siblings, and sometimes whole families are increasingly summoning the courage to search for and develop relationships with their biological sons, daughters, brothers, and sisters.

Pluses and Minuses

There undeniably are pitfalls in "open adoption," an imprecise term applied to an array of arrangements in which birth parents stay involved after placing a child. Some problems derive from the specific personalities or situations of those involved, but many are characteristic of various phases of openness, as everyone tries to deal with emotional uncertainty and, if direct contact is included, to determine their boundaries and sort out their evolving roles. In most cases, the long-term gains are considerable nevertheless, and that's why expanding openness is the central characteristic of the adoption revolution. . . .

The bottom line . . . is that greater openness for adoptees means an upbringing rooted in self-knowledge and truth rather than equivocation or deception; for birth parents, it helps diminish angst and permits grieving, and therefore increases their comfort levels with their decisions; and for adoptive parents, it eases personal insecurities while establishing a steady stream of information for their children and for making critical parenting decisions (based, for example, on the birth family's medical history).

THE PROBLEMS OF OPEN ADOPTION

Mary Beth Style

In the following article, Mary Beth Style writes that while some open adoption experiences may be positive in ideal circumstances, most such arrangements fall short and are susceptible to problems. Open adoption—adoption in which adoptive parents, birth parents, and adopted children stay in regular contact—was designed in part to assist grieving birth mothers who had not come to terms with the relinquishment of a child, Style argues, but the process actually has the reverse effect. Thus, Style claims that open adoption prevents birthmothers from attaining the closure necessary for healing. Open adoptions often lead to conflicts between adoptive parents and birth parents when the terms of contact are violated or misunderstood, Style says. Such arrangements can also be harmful to adopted children, Style says, by introducing difficult concepts before the child has developed to the point of understanding them or by creating confusion for the child about parental roles. Style has been a social worker in the field of adoption for over twenty years and served for nine years as vice president of the National Council for Adoption.

One of the most controversial issues in adoption today is the question of whether there should be contact between birthparents and adopted persons and their families. In the jargon of the day, the more contact the parties have with one another, the more "open" the adoption is. Generally proponents and opponents of contact have a very different philosophical view of adoption. It is important for each individual and family involved in adoption to determine what is right for them. . . .

Birthmothers' Grief

To discuss "open" adoption, it is important to understand how and why the practice began. In the 1970s it became clear to adoption workers that there were women who had placed children for adoption in earlier years who were anguishing over their actions. Many reported that they were told they would forget about the child they placed and would "get over it." They returned to the agencies or other

Mary Beth Style, "Contact Between Birthparents and Adoptive Families," *Adoption Factbook III*, edited by Connaught Coyne Marshner. Washington, DC: National Council for Adoption, 1999. Copyright © 1999 by the National Council for Adoption. Reproduced by permission.

counselors years later to report they had not "gotten over it." Enough of these experiences convinced some in the adoption field that a birthmother did not "get over" an adoption and that they, therefore, needed to make changes in adoption to prevent this continuing pain. It is often repeated that the loss in adoption is different than other losses because the child is still alive and that is why birthmothers cannot recover from it. "Open" adoption was seen as the way to avoid the loss for the birthmothers by providing the birthmother contact with the child who is now a part of another family. The goal was noble—to prevent pain. However, the means were based on an erroneous understanding of the grief process and in many cases, the true cause of the birthmother's pain.

For one thing, proponents of "open" adoption do not understand that it is not the type of loss which determines whether or not someone will be able to resolve the loss positively, but the strengths and resources that each individual possesses or has access to which will make the difference. Most losses we experience in life involve an individual who is still alive. Unfortunately, there is not enough space to discuss the entire healing process here. Basically, resolving the adoption loss for a birthmother requires a realistic understanding of the relationship, or more appropriately, understanding the lack of a parent/ child relationship. Resolution also depends on acquiring the belief that adoption was beneficial to the child, and, most importantly, on forgiving oneself and anyone else involved in the pregnancy or adoption with whom the birthmother may be angry. Perhaps the most important thing is to identify accurately the source of the woman's anguish. This author's experience with birthmothers who express a lack of peace suggests that the source of the disquiet is their continuing shame over the out-of-wedlock pregnancy.

This lack of understanding of grieving and therefore, the attempt to avoid loss through "open" adoption in fact makes it more difficult for birthmothers to achieve a positive resolution. One reason is the message is clear that the birthmother will not recover and so the continuing pain becomes a self-fulfilling prophecy. A University of Texas at Arlington study corroborated what many counselors have witnessed—that "open" adoption appears to prevent closure for women making it impossible to heal. "Biological mothers who know more about the later life of the child they relinquished have a harder time making an adjustment than do mothers whose tie to the child is broken off completely by means of death. Relinquishing mothers who know only that their children still live but have no details about their life appear to experience an intermediate degree of grief."

The Birthmother–Adoptive Parent Relationship

To be sure, many birthmothers in "open" adoption arrangements will report very positive experiences. If all adult parties involved in the adoption (the birthparents and adoptive parents) are: emotionally stable and secure; have a clear understanding of their roles and the child's developmental needs; have compatible personalities; and have similar expectations, an "open" adoption probably can work well. However, those are a lot of variables which must be considered in each case. A common complaint by adoptive families is that the birthmother of their child is too needy and they feel they have adopted her and her problems along with the child. This may happen if the birthmother is depressed, has many problems, and/or feels isolated without any other support network.

A common complaint from birthmothers is that adoptive parents have not held up their end of the bargain for contact. This comes from different expectations from the parties or changing expectations once the adoptive parent becomes a parent. What each person believes parenting to be prior to becoming a parent and the actual experience of parenting is usually quite different. Many prospective adoptive parents will make promises with every intention of complying, but find that the involvement with the birthmother interferes with their need for family boundaries or intense demands on their time and energy by their new baby. The natural interpretation of many birthmothers when this change occurs is to suspect that the adoptive parents conned them in order to adopt the child and stopped caring as soon as the child was in their possession. Dismay over failure to follow agreements has led to the emergence of a movement to put court-enforced agreements in place and has led early advocates of "open adoption" to call for an abandonment of adoption and its replacement by guardianship.

The Child's Perspective

A common concern from the child's perspective is that contact, particularly at a young age, may confuse the child about the mother and father role. It also may place too much attention on the fact of adoption, particularly before a child can understand the concept of adoption. Kathleen Silber and Patricia Martinez Dorner wrote *Children of Open Adoption* to promote the practice of "open" adoption. Two excerpts from their book illustrate this point. "As Alberta Taubert indicates, her three-year-old daughter, Jordan, is able to appropriately use the term birthmother and to realize that she grew in Christy's womb and, in fact, got her curly hair from Christy. Of course, Jordan only has an elementary understanding of adoption." A child of three calling a woman "birthmother" does not indicate that she understands the relationship. Certainly she does not understand genetics and the transmission of "curly hair" through genes.

More disturbing is the discussion of grief in adopted children and the concern that this emphasis on adoption and a birthmother may actually cause stress for a child. Silber and Dorner state "the realization and experience of loss is demonstrated by adopted children at earlier ages than previously believed. The different manifestations of grief are evidenced by the children—we see denial, sadness, and anger. Jennifer's story reflects how denial came into play for this child. At age 4½ Jennifer began to emphatically say that she had not grown in Gloria's womb. Over time, Jennifer's mom had explained her adoption story in simple terms, including that Jennifer had grown in Gloria's womb.

This "theory" of grief in adopted children is inconsistent with the findings of David Brodzinsky, Ph.D., who has done extensive research on children's growing understanding of adoption. His research in this area is consistent with learning theory. Brodzinsky reports that "sometime around 8 to 10 years of age, children begin to understand what relinquishment means. In middle childhood, reflection begins on the adoption process itself. This is a normal part of coping with adoption." Brodzinsky and most other child development experts caution parents in early telling of adoption that children cannot understand the concept of adoption, or for that matter childbearing, in the same way adults do and the information can be distorted in the child's mind. One wonders why this child has had to "emphatically say that she had not grown in Gloria's womb." It seems more likely that this response is not a reaction to her feelings of loss of Gloria, but her confusion and perhaps anger at her mother's insistence that she is not Jennifer's mother. Repeated discussions about birthmothers and adoption with young children will not make them understand it before they are developmentally capable, but may have the effect of overwhelming them.

Therefore, in an "open" adoption relationship, it appears that a child may do fine if his developmental needs are met. In other words, he may have a very close relationship with a birthparent and receive great benefit from the attention and affection of a loving adult in addition to his parents. However, it is an adult's need and contrary to a child's need to explain the relationship in genetic or familial terms. For the child what is essential is the quality of the friendship. Any discussion of roles or relationships may create problems. But to not discuss the relationship would undermine the philosophy of "open" adoption advocates.

Feelings of Rejection

"Open" adoption advocates and others who see adoption as creating pathology have often universalized the expression of some adopted adults to feelings of rejection. The theory is that "open" adoption is supposed to prevent feelings of rejection which proponents mistakenly believe to occur in all adopted persons. Just as "open" adoption was supposed to prevent loss for birthmothers, this attempt at preventing feelings of rejection may actually be causing problems. As the previous examples show, the adults may create confusion and anxiety for a child in their need to show the child is not rejected. This philosophy of adoption requires that the child be aware there is no loss—no rejection. Therefore, the continued birthparent/child relationship must be emphasized to achieve that goal. However the means to that end are contrary to the best interest of children and the end itself is dubious. In reality, if a child has a loving, stable adoptive family, he will not feel rejection. But introducing the notion of rejection when a child has not experienced it and before he can understand the motivations of others will confuse him. For example, in response to a birthmother's need to assure that the child understand that she placed him for adoption because she loved him, not because she did not want him, some children have been told that they were placed for adoption because the birthmother loved them. To an adult it sounds benign enough, but to a literal, consistent child it can raise concerns as his parents have also expressed love and he wonders when he will lose them.

The Open Adoption Dilemma

The reality of adoption . . . is that persons who desire adoption, particularly prospective adoptive parents, may not have many choices of whether to have an "open" adoption or not. Some states require that adoptions arranged by non-agencies be "open" and many agencies have an "open" adoption bias. One of the major reasons couples wishing to adopt, adopt from other countries is because they do not wish to participate in an "open" adoption. The author understands the dilemma for prospective adoptive parents and recommends that they think through all of the issues as carefully as possible. Each family should determine for itself if it feels some contact may be acceptable and if so, how much. It is critical that all parties involved in an "open" adoption have the same philosophy about the adoption and understands that ultimately it is the child's needs which must come first. Any "open" adoption, which is designed to meet the needs of any of the adults, is ripe for problems. The child cannot be expected to heal whatever troubles the adult.

Choosing an Open Adoption Arrangement

Gabrielle Glaser

In the following article, Gabrielle Glaser details an open adoption experience from the perspective of both the birth mother and the couple who adopt her baby, and offers insights into why open adoptions are becoming more prevalent. Glaser states that as many as two-thirds of families hoping to adopt are willing to consider open adoption. While there is little data to determine the effects of open adoption, the article cites one study that found no evidence of harm to the child or parents involved. Gabrielle Glaser is an author and a freelance writer of articles for several newspapers and magazines.

[In the fall of 2003] Mandy Phibbs was a girl in trouble. But her predicament also put her in demand.

Mandy, three months pregnant, had decided to place her baby for adoption. One afternoon, she sat at the suburban Portland [OR] agency she had chosen, sifting through stacks of "Dear Birth Mother" albums filled with notes and photos from prospective parents. All had the comfortable middle-class lives Mandy, then 17, knew she could not provide her child.

The agency had suggested that she set a list of conditions. And so she had: she wanted the parents to be Christians older than 35, married for several years and already raising a child. She ruled out families in Oregon: "Schools are better in Washington," she said.

The most important requirement also created the most complexity: Her baby's family must be within driving distance so that she could continue to be part of her child's life.

She would eventually choose a couple in suburban Seattle to become her baby's parents. They would be with her on the day of delivery and will be in her life from now on.

Open Adoptions on the Rise

Such open adoptions, in which a child develops relationships with both birth parents and adoptive parents, are a striking departure from the secret dealings of a generation ago. Adopting families had scarce information about birth mothers, who after delivery left hospitals with little hope of ever seeing their children again.

The lifelong sorrow, well-publicized, of adoptees and birth parents eventually led to another model. The first open adoptions are believed to have started in California in the early 1980s.

Word of them has slowly spread. Officials are seeing an increase in the number of babies placed for adoption after decades of decline.

"Because of open adoption, more birth mothers are coming to adoption than ever before," said Shari Levine, executive director of Open Adoption & Family Services. The Northwest agency, with headquarters in Portland, facilitates only open adoptions. Its placements have risen from 20 in 1985 to roughly 60 annually in the past few years, Levine said.

No central agency tracks private, domestic adoption statistics. But adoption officials who specialize in open adoption have likewise noted a rise.

Sharon Fitzgerald, of the nonprofit Independent Adoption Center in Pleasant Hill, Calif., said placements at the agency, which has offices nationwide, have increased 8 percent in the past five years.

"What's more important than the raw numbers is that the nature of adoption is changing," said Adam Pertman, author of *Adoption Nation* and executive director of the Evan B. Donaldson Adoption Institute in New York. "Birth mothers are no longer treated simply as baby making machines."

From 1970 to the late 1990s, the number of children placed for adoption declined from roughly 90,000 to 50,000, annually according to a recent issue of "The Future of Children," a policy journal jointly produced by Princeton University and The Brookings Institution. The drop is attributed to the 1973 legalization of abortion, the availability of contraception and the growing acceptance of single parenthood.

Meanwhile, as many as 1 million families hope to adopt, said Brad Imler, president of the nonprofit American Pregnancy Association in Irving, Texas.

And as many as two-thirds of them, officials say, are now willing to welcome women like Mandy into their lives.

The process is not universally accepted. Thomas Atwood, the executive director of the National Council for Adoption in Alexandria, Va., sees problems with open adoption.

"It is not necessarily in the best interest of the child," he says. However, there is little data to determine how openness affects children. He is concerned about cases in which the birth parents' behavior may be damaging to the child.

Harold Grotevant, a University of Minnesota professor who is the co-author of a longitudinal study on open adoption, has found no evidence of harm to the child or to the parents involved.

"Everything we've looked at disagrees with the premise that openness in itself is harmful to children," he said. His studies have found that the open adoption process lessens the grief for birth mothers and was not harmful to the adoptive parents.

It is in the West, with a tradition of independence that lends flexibility to the notion of family, where open adoption predominates.

"In many parts of the East Coast, open adoption is just smoke," Fitzgerald said. "But it's wildfire in the West."

"I Wanted More for My Child"

In her first trimester, Mandy weighed her future as a mother, and it looked bleak. What could she impart to a child? She hadn't yet graduated from high school. Her parents, young themselves, had divorced when she was small.

"They did the best they could," she said, "but I wanted more for my child."

She was raised by her father, Shawn Phibbs, a contractor. But at 16, she chafed at his rules and struck out on her own. She had a bout with drugs and drinking, started seeing a man many years older and moved into his trailer on the coast. She soon discovered she was pregnant.

Not long afterward, she left the man and returned to the home of her father and stepmother, Fawn, 44, in Forest Grove. Fawn, mother of a 24-year-old son, is an advertising agency executive who grew up in foster homes.

Both insisted that Mandy, who hopes to join the Air Force, continue her education, and Shawn, 39, encouraged her to consider an open adoption.

After their own two decades of child rearing, they felt ill-prepared to raise another child. And Shawn told Mandy: "You can't go to college with a baby in your back seat."

Throughout her pregnancy, that crisp sentence became Mandy's mantra.

Abortion was out of the question. She had had one, at 14, and her eyes well up when she thinks about it. She still can't forgive herself for it, she said.

So one by one, she called adoption agencies listed in the yellow pages and met the one she felt accorded her the most respect. Some of them, she said, treated her like she was just a number.

The first "Dear Birth Mother" album Mandy saw was from Jan and Ken Sharp, a suburban Washington couple in their 40s with a 2-year-old son, Sam. As she sorted through all the others, the Sharp family kept drawing her back. Jan, a former teacher, and Ken, an assistant suburban fire chief, seemed to radiate warmth even from the laminated pages.

"There will rarely be a day that I won't think of you and wonder how you are doing," Jan wrote. "Just as you will think of your baby and me, I will always remind this child that they are lucky enough to have two mothers who love (him or her.)" The words were com-pelling—and revealing.

"It wasn't all about her," Mandy said.

Other details hit Mandy just as powerfully. In a photograph of the nursery, Mandy saw the same white crib she had picked out for the baby if she decided to raise the child. In another photo, Mandy spot-ted a pair of papier-mache figures from Mexico. A friend of Jan's had given them to her as souvenirs, and they perched on a living room coffee table.

Mandy recognized them instantly; Fawn had some nearly identical ones in the Phibbs' home.

To Mandy, the figures took on a totemic meaning. They repre-sented the steadiness Fawn, whom Mandy calls her mother, had brought to Mandy's life.

"When I saw those things, I just started bawling," Mandy said. "They were the right ones."

But that didn't help the conflictng feelings Mandy had about the strange relationship that drew them together. The Sharps were unable to have a baby but could educate and care for one. Mandy, 17 and pregnant, was unprepared for motherhood.

"I felt like I didn't deserve my baby," Mandy said.

Rapport with the Adoptive Family

[On] Halloween [2003], Jan was chatting with some relatives when the phone rang. It was the Sharps' caseworker, calling to say an Ore-gon birth mother wanted to meet them.

Jan was stunned—and wary. Nothing in her path to parenthood had been easy. Infertility was painful enough, and adoption was prov-ing no less trying. Sometimes, she wondered if she wasn't destined to remain a teacher, shepherding children to adulthood only in the classroom.

Once the Sharps turned to adoption, they were chosen quickly by a birth mother. But the adoption fell through at the last minute when the father refused to sign termination rights—from prison, no less.

Nine months later, the Sharps adopted Sam after a surprise call. He was 7 weeks old and had been in interim foster care as legalities for-malized from his birth father's home state of South Dakota.

Ken, 46, had a daughter from his first marriage, now 22, and to-gether, he and Jan had Sam.

"Let's count our blessings," he told her. He couldn't bear to see his wife endure any more torment.

But Jan, 41, an energetic woman with expressive hazel eyes, was reared in a large Roman Catholic family in Wisconsin. She couldn't imagine just one child in her life and persuaded Ken to keep their file active at the agency just a few more months. Then the call came.

Within weeks, the Sharps drove to Portland to meet Mandy at the agency. They had instant rapport, and the couple went with Mandy to her obstetrician's appointment.

Jan stood watch over Mandy's gel-covered belly as she peered at the ultrasound screen. A 9 ounce fetus floated peacefully, spine and organs intact.

"It's a girl," the technician announced.

During her pregnancy, people stopped Mandy to ask her what she was having, what she was naming it, and if her nursery was ready. She was blunt with all questioners: "I'm having a girl, I don't have a nursery, and I'm not naming her. Her parents are."

People looked at her strangely, but she didn't care.

"Why lie?" she said. "People look at you like you are a terrible person, but really, it's the opposite. You love your baby so much, you want to do the best thing for it."

Sometimes doubts filtered through, but Mandy considered her reality.

"My baby deserved two parents who didn't fight and the opportunity to go to college. I'm an 18-year-old barista with a high school diploma and no health insurance. How could I support her?"

Adding to the picture was the birth father. . . . He was reluctant to sign off on the adoption, Mandy said, but finally consented.

In late April, Mandy was ready to give birth, and the Sharps drove three hours to the hospital. Only Fawn stayed in the delivery room.

Finally, little Chloe was born. She weighed 6 pounds, 2 ounces.

The First Few Days

Within hours, Mandy asked to sign the papers that would relinquish her parental rights. The birth father came to the hospital to sign them, too, and quickly left. Mandy wanted to do it soon so she could just focus on the baby.

On Chloe's first night, Jan slept with Mandy and Chloe in the hospital room. Mandy didn't want to be alone, and Jan didn't want her to be. So Jan slipped on a sweat suit and climbed onto the room's pullout chair. Whenever Chloe budged in her cot, Mandy woke up and fretted that she needed a bottle. But Jan told her: "Honey, she's just stirring. Go back to sleep."

The next day, Mandy didn't let Chloe out of her sight. She put the baby, swaddled in the hospital receiving blanket, in bed next to her.

"I just wanted her to know how much I loved her," she said. "Knowing I was all she needed, it was perfect. Everything we did was good.

"I'm better off and she's better off, but those first few days." Her voice trails off. "They were so sweet and so perfect."

The goodbye, however, was not. As she prepared to leave the hospital, Mandy held Chloe tightly. She told her how much she loved her and explained her decision.

"I knew it wasn't logical," she said.

Then she dressed her in a flowered cotton outfit and asked the nurse for a duplicate set of footprints. Chloe slept, oblivious to the emotions around her.

Jan and Ken stood by, both hopeful and helpless.

"What do you say to someone?" he asked. "Thanks?"

There is perhaps never so much expectation for a human being as when a newborn leaves the hospital: Tired but glowing new mother, surrounded by flowers and balloons, holds a bundled infant. The baby's face is obscured by a little hat, and it is almost always asleep. But that never stops relatives from snapping dozens of pictures.

In open adoption, though, even that scene is tinged with grief and the sense that perhaps things might have been different.

Tears slid down Jan's face as she took Chloe from the nurse. She kept thinking about Mandy. "Focus on the baby," she told herself.

Once outside, Jan and Ken locked Chloe, snug in her infant seat, into their car. Shawn helped steady his daughter as Fawn loaded her trunk with Mandy's bouquets, the giant birthing ball and a teddy bear.

And like Chloe in the car driven by her father, Mandy slid into the back of the car driven by hers.

As Jan and Ken fastened their seat belts, Jan turned to Ken and said: "This looks good on paper, but it sure doesn't feel right."

Mandy dove beneath the windows so her weeping would be out of sight of the Sharps. She gulped for air like a fish on a boat deck as Fawn stroked her hair.

But she had to compose herself for a meeting at a restaurant with the Sharps and Chloe. Agency officials recommend such "placement ceremonies" after the families leave the hospital. They serve as an emotional punctuation point at the end of one chapter and the beginning of another.

Shawn suggested going to The Spaghetti Factory, a Portland establishment known for its raucous family birthday parties. He thought the restaurant's commotion might detract from the occasion's sadness.

Everyone was exhausted. At the restaurant, Chloe was perched in her car seat between Jan and Mandy. Mandy had no appetite and looked over often to check that the baby was breathing.

Ken and Jan presented Mandy with a gift, a necklace with Chloe's birthstone, a diamond.

The couple had pondered what to give her for weeks. Even now, Ken perhaps still wonders. "What is appropriate?" he asked as he bounced Chloe, now 5 months, on his knee.

"Here we are, with the big pay-off, a beautiful, healthy little girl. After our dinner, we were driving her up to a big celebration with her brother, her grandparents and a whole family of aunts and uncles."

"And poor Mandy," he said. "Mandy was just going back home to her room. Mandy wasn't pregnant any more, she didn't have any doctor's visits anymore, and she was all alone. You can't imagine how awful you feel. Overjoyed you have that baby but awful thinking of what the birth mother is going through."

He was right to wonder. Certainly, the dinner hadn't brought much "closure" for Mandy. That night, Mandy took one look at her room and turned around. Without her belly, without her baby, her own double bed seemed enormous.

So she slept on the living room couch, just outside her parents' room. In her hands, she held the receiving blanket that still smelled like her baby.

The Right Decision for Chloe

During Mandy's pregnancy, Shawn had detached himself from its realities. "She'll give it up and we'll all go on," he thought to himself. A trim, muscular man with a boyish face, Shawn is a recovering alcoholic who has been sober for a decade. As he recalls holding Chloe for the first time, he brushes tears away with his fists. "I just wasn't prepared for how much I'd love her."

As he held his granddaughter, the possibilities, and the past, flashed before him.

"I wasn't the perfect father to Mandy," he said. "With Chloe . . ." He looked outside, unable to finish his sentence.

Now, though, his role was to help his daughter through her grief. Though Mandy had the help of agency counselors, the truth was unavoidable: she had, at least in part, lost her baby. Fawn tried joking that they needed Costco-size supplies of Kleenex, but no one much laughed. Privately, Shawn told her: "Let's just go buy a crib and tell Ken and Jan, 'We're going to raise that baby.'" Fawn replied: "I absolutely agree."

He shakes his head, as if shivering will somehow loose his sadness.

"We're intelligent enough to separate emotions from our actions, but if we'd been given a choice at that moment, we would've grabbed Mandy and Chloe and brought that baby home—and not regretted it to this day."

"It's hard to give part of your family away when you never really had one yourself," Fawn said. "Ken and Jan are giving Chloe the best childhood she can have. Raising a family is hard work, and it's tiring. They're only just starting. They're giving her better than we could give her. Better than Mandy could give her. That's the intellectual reality."

But when babies are involved, emotions often eclipse reason. So the night before the Sharps left for home, Mandy, Fawn and Shawn drove to see Chloe at their hotel room.

Mandy held and fed Chloe and thanked the Sharps again and again. In turn, they thanked her yet again.

"We all knew, in our heart of hearts, that it was the right decision for Chloe, for us to adopt another child, and for Mandy to allow herself to grow into the young woman she could be without the pressures of motherhood," Jan said.

But most everyone knows that "It's-for-the-best" thoughts often feel much like bitter pills. Ken and Jan tried hard to smile as Mandy and her parents said goodbye and stepped out into the warm night.

A few moments later, the sound of Mandy's sobbing drifted up from the parking lot. Jan glanced at Ken. Without a word, they crossed the room, away from the open window.

The Open Arrangement

[In the fall of 2004] Shawn drove Mandy and a friend, Annie, to visit the Sharps.

Mandy and the Sharps have agreed to two visits a year. Sometimes a birth parent and the adoptive family will exceed an agreement if both parties are comfortable. Experts say birth mothers often want to visit more in the first year but will reduce their visits as the grief subsides.

In the best of times, hosts want the house to be clean, the food to be delicious. But when you are receiving the biological family of your baby, the stakes are perhaps higher. In open adoption, etiquette comes with experience alone.

"You wonder: Are we extending ourselves too much? Too little?" Jan asked.

"We know we're good parents and that things are going well," Ken said. "But when the birth family's coming, you want to be on top of your game."

But the meeting was relaxed. Mandy played with Chloe as Annie and Jan looked on. Shawn and Ken watched football on television.

A few hours later, they left. Moments into the trip, Annie discovered she had left her coat. Shawn left the girls at a coffee shop and returned for it.

Shawn recalls that when Ken saw Shawn at the door, he looked anxious—until Shawn said, "Annie forgot her coat."

Ken, though, remembers only finding the jacket and chatting pleasantly with Shawn. The fathers agreed that Mandy was doing well, and Ken saw Shawn off.

"Totally innocuous," he said.

But the contrast in the impressions of that small exchange reveals something greater: Ambivalence will likely hover for years to come, on birthdays, during visits, and as the two families hang their Christmas stockings.

It is perhaps as much a part of the equation as tiny Chloe herself.

Adult Adoptees Should Have Full Access to Their Adoption Records

Bastard Nation

The following article is taken from the manifesto of Bastard Nation, an adoptee rights organization advocating for the rights of adult adoptees to access all government documents (such as original birth certificates) pertaining to their adoptions. To prohibit this access, the group argues, is to deny adult adoptees rights that belong to adults who were not adopted. Bastard Nation claims that adoption records have been sealed in the past to protect birthparents, adoptees, and adoptive parents from feelings of shame associated with adoption, and that keeping records sealed perpetuates negative attitudes toward adoption. The group also rejects arguments that opening adoption records to adult adoptees will invade the privacy of birth parents or result in fewer adoptions or increased abortion rates.

Adoptee birth records are sealed because of an attitude of shame towards adoption. The language in the original laws [that date to the 1930s and 1940s] which sealed adoptee records specifically stated that it was to protect adoptees from the shame and embarrassment of their illegitimate (i.e. Bastard) status. The later justifications we hear for adult adoptees' birth records being sealed are: 1) to protect the birth parent (unspoken assumption—from the shame of the unwanted birth coming back to haunt her); 2) to protect the adoptee (unspoken assumption—from the shame of being reminded that one was born of an unwanted pregnancy); and 3) to protect the adoptive parents (unspoken assumption—from the shame of their infertility). In reality there shouldn't be anything shameful about adoption. Sealed records preclude that possibility.

Bastard Nation explodes the myth of shame by reclaiming the word "bastard" and all of society's myths and fears regarding adoption. We make fun of the unspoken shame, joke about illegitimacy and tell the untold tales of our sisters and brothers which the media

David Ansardi et al., "The Basic Bastard," Bastard Nation: The Adoptee Rights Organization, www.bastards.org, edited by Cynthia Bertrand Holub, 2003. Copyright © 2003 by Bastard Nation. Reproduced by permission.

have not been willing to tackle. We give adult adoptees a place to come and express themselves, share their experiences, read about others like and unlike themselves, find search and reconnection resources and learn how to fight for their rights as adult adoptees. . . .

The Open Records Issue

Adult adoptees in all but five states and two commonwealths in the United States (Kansas, Alaska, Oregon, Alabama, New Hampshire, Puerto Rico and the U.S. Virgin Islands) and in all Canadian provinces are forbidden unconditional access to their original birth certificates. Outmoded Depression-era laws create "amended" birth certificates that replace the names of the adoptee's biological parents with those of the adoptive parents as well as frequently falsify other birth information. The adoptee's original birth certificate and records of adoption are permanently sealed in closed records states by laws passed largely after World War II. These laws are a relic of the culture of shame that stigmatized infertility, out-of-wedlock birth and adoption. Even those adoptees now being raised in open adoptions, in which there is some contact between birth and adoptive families, are not allowed access to their original birth records when they reach adulthood.

In Scotland adoptee records have been open since 1930 and in England since 1975. Sweden, The Netherlands, Germany, South Korea, Mexico, Argentina and Venezuela are only a few of the many nations that do not prevent adult adoptees from accessing their own birth records. The United States and Canada lag far behind the rest of what we used to call the "Free World" in opening closed birth and adoption records to those to whom they pertain. This is largely because well-funded and well-connected lobbies representing certain adoption agencies and lawyers have a vested interest in keeping adoptee records closed. These special interest groups want to continue to deprive adult adoptees of their rights, presumably to prevent the disclosure of controversial past practices such as baby-selling, coercion and fraud which are now hidden by state-sanctioned secrecy.

While many adoptees search for their biological relatives to discover the answers to questions regarding medical history and family heritage, all adoptees should be able to exercise their right to obtain the original government documents of their own birth and adoption whether they choose to search or not. At stake are the civil and human rights of millions of American and Canadian citizens. To continue to abrogate these rights is to perpetuate the stigmatization of illegitimacy and adoption, and the relegation of an entire class of citizens to second-class status.

A History of Sealed Records

Adoption records and original birth certificates have not always been sealed. Sealing records is, in fact, a relatively recent development in

our nation's history. Birth certificates themselves c‐
quired in the first decades of [the twentieth] ce‐
were marked "legitimate" or "illegitimate" in mo‐
of the stigma associated with illegitimacy, they were sea‐
lic, but were available to the adoptee upon majority. The
birth certificate, which names the adoptive parents in the place o‐
birth parents, was first proposed by two Registrars of Vital Statistics in
1931 and was utilized by most states by the end of World War II. In the
decades leading up to World War II, court records and original birth
certificates were sealed to the public, the explicit reason given being to
protect the adoptive family from exposure to embarrassment or even
blackmail regarding the illegitimate origins of the adoptee, or in cases
where the adoptee had not been told of the adoption to keep that the
prerogative of the adoptive parents. Many states sealed adoption
records to birth parents as well, fearing their interference in the life of
the adoptee. Nowhere in any of these original statutes is there any ref-
erence to the protection of birth parents' privacy.

Records were sealed to all parties in most states after World War II,
largely on the recommendation of professional social work organizations and adoption agencies. These statutes, however, usually included the provision that records could be opened by court order, and
in fact many states still have provisions on the books allowing release
of records such as the adoption decree to the adoptive parents, or allowing the records to remain unsealed at the adoptive parents' request. Even in states where this is not officially codified, many adoptive parents routinely obtain records with the names of the birth
parents on them at the time of the adoption, or can obtain them by
request. There are a number of reasons for this sealing. Social workers
lobbied for greater "confidentiality" as a way of increasing their own
power and boosting the prestige of their profession. The postwar demographic boom in single pregnancy saw a change in the demographic composition of birth mothers from primarily married or divorced working-class women who relinquished their usually older
children for economic reasons, to younger, more broadly middle-class
unmarried women who relinquished their children in infancy. The
paradigm of the unwed mother had changed from her being congeni-
tally feeble-minded to being neurotic and therefore curable; it was
deemed best for there to be a complete and early break between
mother and relinquished child for the sakes of both. The child was no
longer seen as innately tainted by its illegitimate origins, but as a
blank slate ready for the adoptive parents to write upon. The new,
amended birth certificate and the permanently sealed original fos-
tered the illusion of a brand-new family with no prior or potentially
disruptive future connections to the birth family, a "selling device"
for agencies to attract adoptive parents. It was assumed that "well-
adjusted" adoptees would have no interest in their origins.

While most states sealed their records in the 1940s and 1950s, some states did not do so until much later, with Pennsylvania sealing original birth certificates only in 1984 and Alabama in 1991; by 1998 only Kansas and Alaska still allowed unconditional adoptee access. In November 1998 the voters of Oregon approved the Bastard Nation–inspired ballot initiative, Measure 58, which made Oregon the first state to open, unconditionally, previously sealed records to adult adoptees. After a series of unsuccessful court challenges, the law finally went into effect on May 30, 2000. Also in May 2000, with the full support of the Governor and Lt. Governor, a unanimous vote in the House and only two dissenting votes in the Senate, Alabama reversed its 1991 sealed records law and granted unrestricted access to original birth and adoption records to that state's adult adoptees. This was accomplished through the lobbying efforts of Alabamians Working for Adoption Reform and Education (AWARE), with the support of Bastard Nation and other adoption reform organizations. . . .

Conditional Access to Records

Many states have intermediary systems, which authorize an agency worker or court-appointed agent to access the adoptee's records and to perform a search for biological relations on their behalf. Permission for contact with and/or divulgence of identifying information to the adoptee is solicited from the birth parent, and the adoptee is furnished with no information or records if the birth parent declines. This system takes all control from the hands of the adoptee and is designed to facilitate reunions rather than restore adoptee rights.

Contact vetoes, whereby the birth parent may file a statement that they do not wish to be contacted by the adoptee and by which the adoptee must abide or be subject to criminal penalties, are a violation of an adoptee's right to due process and equal protection under the law. Conditional access legislation in the form of the contact veto implies that adoptees and birth parents are not capable of handling adult contact. If either party in an adoption does not wish contact, they can simply say no, as in any other adult situation. If they feel they are being unduly harassed, they can use the same remedies at their disposal as other citizens. Traditional no-contact orders and orders of protection are issued via court order after a person has demonstrated a pattern of threatening or abusive behavior. Even then the person who has the order issued against them has the right to answer and face their accuser in a court of law. Contact vetoes, however, are issued based solely on the adoptive status of an individual and are without legal recourse or appeal. In open records states where no contact veto exists (Kansas, Alaska, Oregon and Alabama), there are no reports of incidents that would demonstrate a necessity for special protection of the birth family.

Contact veto systems, which are opposed by Bastard Nation, exist in North America in British Columbia, Colorado and Tennessee and sprang from similar laws originating in the Australian territories, most notably when New South Wales passed its Adoption Information Act of 1990. Queensland has a similar veto law. Violating a contact veto in New South Wales carries monetary penalties as well as jail time. Similar penalties exist in the veto systems present in North America.

In contrast, a contact preference system does not legally bind the adoptee to abide by the request of the person filing their contact preference form (CPF). Such a system simply permits a birth parent to express their wishes concerning contact and does not place a condition on access or criminalize an adoptee unfairly. CPFs are an acceptable compromise to Bastard Nation and were written into Bastard Nation–supported open records laws in both Oregon and Alabama as amendments to forestall worse provisions being added.

It can be dangerous to write a contact preference system into proposed legislation from the beginning, however, as such a scheme can quickly be amended into a veto. Amending proposed open records legislation with a contact preference provision should only be done when activists and their sponsor have a close and trusting relationship and when the legislation can be assured of a better chance of passage with the sole addition of the contact preference amendment. Activists are encouraged not to include CPFs in ballot measure texts, but rather once an open records measure has passed to use the CPF to head off any more dangerous legislative tinkering.

Age of access is another issue which activists often have to contend with in lobbying open records legislation or writing ballot measures. There are three common ages of majority used in North America upon which a person acquires all (or most of) the rights and responsibilities of being an adult. These are eighteen, nineteen and twenty-one. Bastard Nation therefore supports unconditional access legislation that sets the age of eligibility at any of these three levels. In other parts of the world, Bastard Nation supports setting age of access to correspond with a country's general trend in age of majority law. . . .

Do Birth Parents Have a Right to Privacy?

One of the main concerns raised by those who oppose opening records to adult adoptees is that doing so violates their birth parents' right to privacy. Open records proponents have long argued that there is no right to privacy that extends to birth parent anonymity, and on February 11, 1997, the Sixth Circuit Court of Appeals handed down a decision confirming this view. [*106 F.3d 703 (6th Cir. 1997)*]

In 1996 the Tennessee legislature passed a law granting certain adult adoptees access to their original birth certificates, subject to contact vetoes and significant exception clauses. The law was halted by a court injunction when a group of birth mothers, adoptive parents and an adoption agency filed suit claiming the law violated their constitutional rights under both the Tennessee and Federal Constitution. The federal case ended in 1998 when the United States Supreme Court declined to overrule the Appeals Court ruling in favor of the defendants and open records. The courts rejected the plaintiffs' claim that their right to privacy was infringed upon, stating, "A birth is simultaneously an intimate occasion and a public event—the government has long kept records of when, where, and by whom babies are born. Such records have myriad purposes, such as furthering the interest of children in knowing the circumstances of their birth." The judges of the Sixth Circuit Court further found that "if there is a federal constitutional right of familial privacy, it does not extend as far as the plaintiffs would like." The court also cited a 1981 decision in which the appeals court found that "the Constitution does not encompass a general right to nondisclosure of private information." More directly, the Court found that the interest of an adoptee to know who his or her birth parents are is "an interest entitled to a good deal of respect and sympathy."

The right to privacy, an implicit right that is not found specifically within the United States Constitution, requires case law to flesh it out and define it further. Our nation's courts have spoken clearly that the right to privacy does not extend to withholding birth information from the very person to whom it primarily pertains—the adoptee.

Birth parents could have had no reasonable expectation of anonymity. The original birth certificate is sealed when the adoption is finalized in court, not when the birth mother signs relinquishment papers. A child relinquished but never adopted has an unsealed birth certificate. If protection of the birth mother were intended, the original birth certificate would be sealed upon termination of her legal relationship to the child, not at the beginning of the legal relationship of the adoptive family. Nearly all states have provisions for opening adoption or birth records for good cause without the consent or even notification of the birth parent. Birth mothers signed irrevocable relinquishment forms, but there have been no contracts produced promising that an adoptee's original birth record would remain sealed.

Despite the finding that birth parent privacy rights do not extend as far as keeping their names secret from adoptees, opponents of open records have continued to claim that some birth parents, particularly women, would be harmed emotionally if they were to be contacted by a relinquished child who had reached the age of majority. In addition, some reproductive rights advocates believe that permanently sealed birth records should be an option for pregnant women who choose not to raise a child.

In reality their adult children, raised by others, are not the enemies of birth parents. Our laws and policies should not deprive one group of their rights in order to protect others from possibly having to face the consequences of their past choices. In the event that an adoptee chooses to contact a birth parent, both people should consider the feelings and concerns of the other. When birth records are opened to adult adoptees, a woman who relinquishes an infant will have eighteen to twenty-one years to decide how to answer a possible phone call from that adult child. Even today, with records still sealed in most states in the United States, birth parents must consider their responses to being found, since a network of search consultants has arisen to circumvent sealed records. Most birth parents are happy to be contacted by their adult children. A right to privacy that prevents the disclosure of birth parents' names to adult adoptees does not exist in law or in the real world.

There is no real conflict of interest between birth parents and adoptees. The apparent conflict is a creation of the opposition to open records, primarily a section of the adoption industry which fears its past misdeeds coming to light. . . .

Access to Records—the Effect on Abortion and Adoption Rates

Many opponents of open records for adult adoptees have claimed, with no basis in fact, that young pregnant women would choose abortion over adoption if their relinquished children would be able to discover their birth mothers' names in eighteen years' time. They also claim that open records would lead to a decline in adoption rates because potential adoptive parents would be discouraged by a system in which their children would no longer be permanently denied their own birth records. Both these claims belong in the realm of myth and propaganda and may be countered by statistical evidence to the contrary. While there are many factors that determine abortion rates in various states and countries, and it cannot be claimed that open records bears a causal relation to lower abortion rates. It can, however, be shown that abortion rates are not higher and are in fact lower in open records states than in states with sealed records. It can likewise be shown that states and countries with open records have not seen a decline in adoption rates.

The abortion rates for Alaska and Kansas, which have long granted adult adoptees unconditional access to their original birth certificates, were both lower in 1996 than the rate for the United States as a whole—14.6 and 18.9 abortions, respectively, for every 1000 women between the ages of fifteen and forty-four, while the national abortion rate was 22.9.

In Alabama, which opened records to adult adoptees in August 2000, the total number of abortions declined by 1.3% (from 13,533 to 13,382) during the first full year of open records compared to the previous year when records were closed for the majority of the year. Abortions among girls and women under eighteen have been declining since 1998. The sharpest year-to-year decline actually occurred in

2001 (down 10.9%, from 1,029 to 917), the first full year the records were open in Alabama.

Data compiled by the Alan Guttmacher Institute showing the number and rate of abortions in England and Wales by year for 1961 through 1987 indicate a continuous increase in abortions and abortion rates from 1961 through 1973. In 1974 through 1976, when the opening of adoption records was discussed in Parliament and put into effect, abortions and the abortion rate decreased.

The National Center for Court Statistics reported that the 1992 rate of adoptions per thousand live births were 31.2 nationally, 53.5 in Alaska and 48.4 in Kansas, two open records states, but lower in surrounding states with sealed records laws (CO, 26.0; MO, 27.5; NE, 42.4; and OK 47.6).

Barbara Flett, Registrar of the New South Wales Registry of Births, Deaths and Marriages, issued a declaration submitted for evidence in the Tennessee conditional records access case, *Doe v. Sundquist* which showed the numbers of adoptions in New South Wales from 1970 through 1995. The New South Wales Adoption Information Act 1990, which became fully effective on April 2, 1991, made original birth certificates accessible by right to adoptees. The data from the Registry of Births, Deaths and Marriages set forth in Ms. Flett's letter show that adoptions peaked in 1972 and then began a decline which has continued steadily to the present day. Prior to the unsealing of adoption records in 1991, adoptions had declined from 4,564 in 1972 to 688 in 1990, a decline of 85 percent. The rate of decline after 1990 shows no significant change from the previous decline and indicates that the opening of adoption records had no measurable effect on the numbers of adoptions.

Annual adoption figures for England and Wales for the years 1960 through 1984, taken from official publications of the United Kingdom Registrar General and the United Kingdom Office of Population Censuses and Surveys, for non-parental (i.e. non-step parent or intrafamilial) adoptions by couples in England and Wales declined continuously from a peak of 14,641 in 1968 down to 1984, which appears to be the last year for which these data were published. From the start of the decline in 1968 until 1976, when adoption records were unsealed, the relevant adoptions declined from 14,641 to 4,777, a decline of 67 percent in eight years; in the following eight years, after the records were unsealed, these adoptions declined to 2,910, a decline of only 39 percent. If the unsealing of adoption records had any effect in England and Wales, therefore, it was to reduce the decline in adoptions, i.e. to increase adoptions over the numbers that otherwise would have been the case.

Adoptive Parents Should Help Their Children Reunite with Birth Parents

Lorna Collier

In the following article, reporter Lorna Collier relates some of the various emotions involved when an adoptee initiates a search for his or her birth parents. Collier cites those who believe reunions with birth parents can help adoptees dispel notions of an idealized birth family and can give satisfaction by answering questions about an adoptee's identity and traits. At the same time, Collier notes, reunions can be sources of anxiety for adoptive parents, who may feel jealousy or insecurity about the role a birth family may play after the reunion or may feel excluded during the search and reunion process itself. The article suggests that adoptive parents should be supportive of the adoptee's search, but their degree of involvement in the search process can vary. Collier is a Chicago-area freelance writer who contributes to the *Chicago Tribune*.

Linda Strodtman always knew that one day, the two children she and her husband had adopted as newborns would want to meet their birth mothers. [In 2001,] Strodtman helped make that happen to the delight of her children—and the consternation of some of her friends.

"They cannot understand this, why I'm not uncomfortable," said Strodtman, 57, a nursing professor in Ann Arbor, Mich., who adopted Andrew, now 18, and Susan, 15, through The Cradle, a Chicago adoption agency.

"They think I should feel threatened. No way do I," said Strodtman. Instead, she said, she believes her family has been enriched by the experience. Her children are "at better peace," no longer worrying and wondering about their birth families, but rather enjoying relationships with newfound siblings as well as discovering more about the missing pieces in their backgrounds.

The reunions—which have taken place by letter and phone, not yet in person—also have not damaged or diminished the relationship Strodtman has with her children.

"If anything, it has brought us closer together," said Susan Strodtman, who began the search for her birth mother with Linda's help last summer, using post-adoption resources offered by The Cradle as well as information Linda discovered on the Internet. Susan spoke with her birth mother on the phone for the first time [on] Mother's Day [2001].

Adoptive parents today are increasingly being faced with the prospect of their children reuniting with their birth families, as open adoption has become more common and Internet searches more viable. Yet not all adoptive parents are as worry-free as Strodtman; for many, the idea of a birth parent entering the picture raises a disquieting swirl of emotions, including fear that they will lose their place in their child's heart, as well as confusion over what their role in the search and reunion should be.

"You say you don't have any, but at some level there is a certain amount of jealousy," said Joyce Jones, a Wheeling saleswoman who recently tracked down her 33-year-old adopted daughter's birth mother. (Jones asked that her real name not be used to protect her family's privacy.)

"We all have our own amount of insecurity," said Jones. "I knew [my daughter's birth mother] could never be her mother, but on some level, she is. I raised [my daughter], I took care of her her whole life, but I didn't give birth to her."

Jones fought off her fears and went on to make the initial contact with her daughter's birth mother for her daughter, a decision she has not regretted.

Yet her initial concerns are typical of those held by many adoptive parents, said Julie Jarrell Bailey, co-author of *The Adoption Reunion Survival Guide*.

Drawing Closer

"Reunion can be a difficult time for many, many adoptive parents," said Bailey, herself an adoptive mother of three boys as well as a biological mother who gave her daughter up for adoption, then reunited with her two decades later.

Although many adoptive parents worry that their relationship with their adopted child will suffer if the child finds his or her birth parents, studies have repeatedly shown that the opposite is more likely to occur. As with the Strodtman family, when adoptive parents support their child in a search, the parents and children usually wind up even closer than before, experts say.

"The search process creates an opportunity for deepening the bond between adoptee and parent," said Cheryl Rampage, senior therapist at the Family Institute at Northwestern University in Evanston, which offers classes and counseling to help parents and their children handle adoption issues. "The best searches I know about have been a collaborative effort between the adoptee and his or her [adoptive] parent."

Sometimes, the reunion helps an adopted child put to rest the fantasy of a perfect, idealized "real" mother or "real" father, said Bailey, clearing the way for a more honest, deeper relationship with the adoptive parents.

Family Traits

Many adopted children also appear to be helped by finally getting answers to lifelong questions about their roots. Strodtman said she believes her children are happier now that they have seen that certain talents and traits—Andrew's musical gifts, Susan's love of animals—are shared by biological family members. Susan also has discovered that her hair and eye color come from her birth mother.

"It was a neat experience," said Andrew, who had his first contact with his birth mother in February [2001]. "I've been learning about all the traits I get from my mother and father's side. . . . My birth parents will not replace my 'parent' parents, but they occupy a special place [in my life]."

Given that adolescence is typically a time of questioning identity, being able to see their reflections in family genes can be a comfort, say some adoptive parents.

"I saw that my daughter was never going to be a totally happy person until she resolved a lot of these questions in her mind," said Jones. "She seemed to have a real need for that connection."

It is relatively rare for adoptive parents to be in charge of the search for their child's parents. About 5 percent of those searching for biological kin in a . . . survey were adoptive parents, according to Melisha Mitchell, field representative of the Illinois branch of the American Adoption Congress.

A Proper Role for Adoptive Parents

Mitchell found that 37 percent of the adoptees perceived their adopted parents as being "extremely supportive of their desires to seek out their biological roots." However, 30 percent were thought to be "opposed to the search." Another third were considered neutral, never having expressed any particularly positive or negative opinions.

Catherine Weigel Foy, a social worker and director of graduate education at the Family Institute, advises adoptive parents to support their child's wishes and to grant permission for a search.

"It's thought that a lot of adoptees don't search because they fear hurting or betraying their adoptive parent," she said.

Some adoptive parents support their child so much in the search that they make the first contact with the birth parent, usually to protect the child from the pain of rejection. However, some experts say this level of involvement is not usually a good idea.

"Adoptive parents need to step back and let their child lead the search and reunion process," Bailey said. "I believe that it's entirely appropriate—if requested by the child—for a parent to be in the same room when the child makes that first phone call, or to proofread a letter the child writes to his birth parent.

"However, for the parent to make the phone call, or write the letter is, in my opinion, crossing over from being supportive to being controlling and/or overprotective."

Even if the reunion does not turn out well, psychologists today generally are in favor of adoption searches, said Rampage, believing it is better "for adoptees not to live with this permanent fantasy, wondering who were these people. Even if the story is tragic, it may be better for some adoptees to know this, rather than live under the shadow of doubt."

However, due to the possibility of negative results, Rampage said reunions typically are not recommended for children until they are at least in late adolescence.

"I think the child's ability to understand the possible consequences [before late adolescence] is extremely limited," she said.

Foreign Roots

Jan Carpenter, 47, is a Chicago stay-at-home mother to a 3½-year-old daughter adopted in China; she expects another daughter from China . . . , and plans to bring her older daughter along on the trip, partly as a way to show her daughter where she came from.

Several years ago, Carpenter, who is adopted, reunited with her biological family, with the support of her adoptive parents, whom she said were always open with her about her adoption and provided her with what information they had.

"I think it's so important if a child wants to know information about their biological history, either from their parents or through a search, that the parent is comfortable with the subject and is able to nurture them through their questions and/or a search," said Carpenter. "In my mind, that support is a way of respecting the individuality and history of that child."

Since her reunion, Carpenter has kept in touch with her birth relatives, some of whom her parents also were able to meet. She said the process brought her closer to her adoptive parents "as being the ones who loved me through my life."

Anxieties and Exclusion

However, adoptive parents should realize that sometimes in a reunion, the adoptee and newly found birth family experience a period of enthrallment with each other—a "honeymoon stage," during which the adoptive parent may feel shut out, said Bailey.

For example, she said, "I have a friend whose daughter's birth family found her. They were running across the country making plans to meet. The adoptive mom said to me, 'I feel so crushed. I feel so left out of everything.'"

Bailey advises adoptive parents to communicate their frustration to their child, but also to be patient and give their child space during this honeymoon stage.

Eventually, said Bailey, the child will come back to the relationship, which is what occurred with her friend, who now is busy helping her daughter plan a wedding.

"I think it's important for the adoptive parents to be there, even if only in the shadows," said Bailey.

"The adoptive parents are the real parents. If they have had a good relationship all their lives, it's not going to change just because the child meets a biological connection. This gives the entire family the opportunity to expand their circle," she said.

Karen Bevers, 61, helped her son, 36, find his birth mother in Illinois . . . by using the Internet. Since then, her son—raised as an only child—has learned he has two sisters and a brother, and has frequent contact with his birth family.

Bevers said that adoptive parents whose kids want to find their birth parents "have nothing to fear. If they've had a loving, bonding relationship with their child all these years, they should want their child to have the answers, and want their grandchildren to have medical information and know their heritage. It's their right.

"There is a chance the reunion might not go well, but then nothing in life is guaranteed. There needs to be closure and peace in everyone's heart."

Younger Adoptees Also Need Answers

Rather than attempting a reunion with a child's birth parents, adoptive parents of younger children seeking information about their biological parents should use other means—conversation, reading books about adoption or therapy—to "help their child accept their adopted status, accept the loss of their original family and feel comfortable with the family they have now," said . . . Rampage. . . .

Susan Stein, a Chicago mother of two adopted children who asked that her real name not be used to protect their privacy, has had to try to answer her 8-year-old adopted daughter's repeated questions about her birth mother, even though she has little information to give her, because the adoption was closed.

One of the few details Stein has about her daughter's birth is the name of the hospital where she was born. One day, after making arrangements with the hospital's social work staff, Stein took her daughter to the hospital for a visit.

"The nurse on duty was an older woman who had been working

there a number of years," said Stein. "She showed us the nursery and told my daughter, 'I can't say for sure, but I possibly could have taken care of you.'"

Stein took a picture of her daughter with the nurse, as well as photos of the nursery and the outside of the hospital.

"Then we wrote a story about our trip to memorialize what we had done and to help her have some record," said Stein. "What I hope to do one of these days is make a scrapbook for her of the photographs and the story, so that she begins to have a piece of something she can hold onto for herself."

The visit seems to have helped quiet some of her daughter's concerns, said Stein, who knows, however, that these questions will more than likely resurface. When they do, said Stein, she wants to make sure her daughter knows she can come to her and her husband with whatever is troubling her.

"My goal with her is to make her feel confident that we, her parents, are going to be fine," said Stein. "Whatever she decides to do, that it's not threatening to us; that we love her and that we understand her feelings of pain on the subject. What I've tried to say to her is that it makes me sad that she is sad, but it doesn't make me sad because she's talking about it."

Stein has told her daughter she will help her search for her birth family when she is older.

CHAPTER 5

PERSONAL STORIES OF ADOPTION

Contemporary Issues
Companion

A Daughter and Birth Mother Reunite and End the Uncertainty in Their Lives

Susan Freinkel

Mary Anne Duffy knew she had been adopted, but she often felt distressed by the physiological and personality differences between her and her adoptive family, as writer Susan Freinkel explains in the following selection. Psychiatrists refer to Mary Anne's feelings as "genealogical bewilderment," and say that this phenomenon can be responsible for feelings of emptiness or uncertainty in some adoptees who have not reunited with their birth parents or lack any information about them. Freinkel explains that Mary Anne's birth mother, Joanne, also thought often of the child she had given up and felt a void in her own life for want of information about her. When the two eventually met, Freinkel reports, they discovered striking similarities in their lives, and each felt a sense of completeness that had been missing. The following article cites research in psychology that lends credence to the existence of a strong, immediate bond and familiarity between relatives reunited as adults. Freinkel is a freelance writer based in San Francisco, California.

Most of us take our geneology for granted. Even if no one's taken the time to outline the family tree, we are still nourished by a sense of our roots. The knowledge that you have your mother's red hair or your grandfather's musical ability, or that your great-grandmother took a steamer from Minsk to New York, becomes as intangibly a part of yourself as your shadow.

Imagine, then, lacking any such knowledge, any sense of a genetic connection to another living soul. Imagine never seeing a face that reflects your features, that can tell you where you come from and where you may go. You might feel as if you barely cast any shadow at all.

So it was for Mary Anne Duffy, who was five weeks old on the raw November day in 1942 that Luther and Mary Replogle brought her home from the hospital. Luther, or Rep as everyone called him, was a widower with a daughter from his first marriage, and when he wed Mary, she was in her late forties and no longer able to bear children of her own. Mary Anne always knew she was adopted, and as she grew up, she also felt something else: "I wasn't part of the family. I had the last name. I had the relatives. They treated me nicely. It just wasn't *my* family, if that makes sense."

Outwardly she lacked for nothing. The family lived in a large Tudor filled with books and art and music in the prosperous Chicago suburb of Oak Park. Time was spent at the country club, summers at a private club in Michigan. She sailed and rode horseback and spent hours in the backyard playhouse that was the envy of the neighborhood kids. But with her parents often away and a sister seven years older, she was lonely.

Growing up, Mary Anne's parents told her that they didn't have to have her, that she was *chosen*. As a child the story was comforting; it made her feel special. "I was proud of that," she recalls, laughing. "I imagined myself lined up in this long window of babies, and they saw me and said, 'Oh, she's got blond hair and blue eyes. She's cute; let's take her.'"

Genealogical Bewilderment

And yet, as she got older, she began to think her parents had made the wrong choice. She was a poor student in a family of intellectuals, never able or wanting to match the A's her sister Betsy so effortlessly brought home. She was a tomboy, forever frustrating her refined and beloved mother's efforts to raise a little lady. She was stubborn and argumentative, traits that drove her father particularly crazy.

But the most telling difference, the one that blared the presence of outside genes, was this: In a family of thin people, Mary Anne was hopelessly fat—a chubby toddler who became a plump girl and then a chunky teen who had to have some of her clothes custom-made. Her bulk infuriated her father. For years he insisted on weighing her daily. She sometimes felt he despised her for being fat, and each added cell of adipose deepened her conviction that he loved Betsy best.

There is a term in adoption circles, "genealogical bewilderment," used by psychiatrist H.J. Sants in 1964 to explain the distress he'd seen in some of his patients who'd been adopted. The condition didn't just apply to some adoptees, Sants said, but potentially to anyone who lacked knowledge of one or both parents. "The resulting . . . confusion and uncertainty," he wrote, "fundamentally undermines his security and thus affects his mental health."

In the highly politicized field of adoption research, that point is much debated. The bulk of adoptive families are loving and successful, and studies comparing adoptees and people raised by their biological parents find that while adoptees are more likely to be troubled during childhood and adolescence, by adulthood the differences have mostly washed out. No one, however, would dispute Sants's basic idea: Not knowing anything about one's birth parents can complicate the already-complicated process of growing up. And among the many factors that appear to make a difference in whether an adopted child thrives without such knowledge are how closely a child resembles the adoptive family in looks, abilities, and temperament, and how well the adoptive family deals with the differences.

Sants likened the genealogically bewildered to the fairy-tale ugly duckling, the baby swan hatched in a nest of ducks who weren't prepared to accept him as one of their own. As Sants pointed out, the ducks "did not know his genealogy. Consequently, they could not understand the significance of his skills or envisage his potentials." Until the ugly duckling could find his clan—could feel the tug of genes and test the pull of the heart—he could never know what he truly was: a swan.

Sometimes life's lessons are fairy-tale simple.

Lacking Roots

Who were Mary Anne's birth parents? Whatever her adopted parents knew, they couldn't or wouldn't fill in the blanks. So Mary Anne learned to fashion her own private answers. For a while she imagined Rita Hayworth was her true mother, after learning they shared the same birthday. It wasn't until she was in high school that she raised the subject with Mary. Would you mind if I looked for my natural mother? she asked, having chosen the words carefully. She could feel Mary's sadness from across the room. You'll have to wait until you're 18 before you can try to get your records, Mary replied, then added softly, but it would break my heart. Mary Anne, who adored her mother, never asked again.

Lacking answers, lacking roots, Mary Anne detected that in the place where a full sense of her self could be nourished, there grew instead . . . a void. "There was just always this empty spot there, this sense of not really knowing who I was," says Mary Anne, voicing a feeling often expressed by adoptees.

"It's not that adopted people don't have an identity; of course they do," says Joyce Pavao, a Cambridge, Massachusetts, psychologist who often works with adoptees and herself was adopted. "But a very fundamental piece of who they are and where they come from has been left off. When they do art therapy, they draw holes or mazes with question marks in the middle."

Mary Anne, however, spent most of her adult life ignoring the question marks, fearing the answers might lead only to rejection. She married at 18, a disastrous union to an older man that lasted a scant five years. She raised their twins, a son and a daughter, on her own. At age 26 she weathered the heartbreak of Mary's death, then felt the relief, after so many years of conflict, of Rep's death when she was 41. She pursued a string of unhappy relationships with uncaring men while keeping friends at a distance. All the while the void persisted, hollowing her out and enveloping her as surely as the shapeless tent dresses she wore to hide her ballooning weight, which once hit 385 pounds.

She was well into her forties before she began to make peace with herself. And in 1991 she even remarried, something she had never imagined doing until she met Chuck Duffy, a stout social worker with a gentle manner, a puckish face, and a love of all things Irish. "He's the first man I was ever 100 percent honest with," Mary Anne says. Then in 1993, shortly after her 51st birthday, she learned she had breast cancer. The surgery and subsequent chemotherapy and radiation went well, but something inside her had clicked. She began wondering again about her heritage, worrying that she might have inherited, and passed on, cancer-prone genes. A few months later, Chuck was watching the local news when a story came on about a new Illinois program to help adoptees with medical needs find their birth parents. He tucked the number into their address book. He knew finding her birth mother would help Mary Anne—and not just with her medical problems. But Chuck is not a pushy man, and he knew his wife was not one to be pushed. So every few months he'd gently ask, Have you thought about calling? Yeah, she'd reply, I'm thinking about it.

Mary Anne's Search Begins

Finally, one fall morning in 1995, Mary Anne dug out the scrap of paper and called the state's official search program.

At first Mary Anne told herself she was searching simply for her medical history. The logic was compelling, especially when her cancer recurred in mid-1997 and she needed to undergo a double mastectomy. But gradually, as the search progressed, she had to admit to herself that she sought more than dry facts. She wanted to hear a voice; she wanted to see a face. Late 1997 brought the call she'd waited for: Her birth mother had been located.

Mary Anne had no idea where to begin when she sat down to write that first letter. And she can't remember now what she did say, besides briefly describing her life and her decision to take up the search. "I didn't want to take a chance of coming on too strong," Mary Anne recalls. "I think I signed off with something noncommittal like 'bye for now' or 'hope to hear from you soon.'"

The response back was equally hesitant. "Hello," it began—a nervous wave across the decades. Then in broad outlines, the letter laid out the story Mary Anne had hungered to hear. The accompanying medical records showed no family history of breast cancer, to Mary Anne's relief. Still, Mary Anne wanted to learn so much more. Next thing she knew, she was calling one Joanne Munoz in western Idaho.

The voice at the other end of the line was deep and quavery.

Joanne had trouble speaking because of a recent stroke. Mary Anne tried to be restrained. "I told her I had received the medical records, but I had some more questions." In truth, her thirst for details could not be contained: One question after another tumbled out. And though she didn't even realize that it was what she most needed to know, she found herself asking, Did you ever try to find me? Her 74-year-old mother didn't even have to think. I always wanted to try to find you, she said, but I was afraid of disrupting your life. I *always* wondered about you—where you were, how you were.

A Birth Mother's Story

How to explain the ties of family? To what extent are we compelled by the relentless logic of bloodlines, a less rational arithmetic of the heart, or some intricate formula fusing both? However one tries to answer these questions in the abstract, each individual's story makes its own case. Whatever the reasons, Joanne Munoz's story was a mirror of Mary Anne's. Since Joanne had let Mary Anne go, each had been shadowed by the same yearning, the same indescribable sense of loss that nothing could fill.

Joanne was a high school junior in suburban Chicago, a heavy girl with an easy laugh and a talent for drawing almost anything, when she got pregnant. The father of the child was a tall air force lieutenant she spent a weekend with and who then dropped out of her life. All she could remember about him was his name, John.

Her parents were mortified. Her father, a career soldier who always seemed disappointed by his only daughter, insisted that she give the child up. He covered up the truth so well that even her younger brother thought she was away at boarding school when she left home. In fact, she was sent to live in nearby Oak Park with a family who wouldn't let her go outside, even for walks. When the baby was born, she didn't get a chance to hold her or even see her. But she couldn't just let the child fade away; she wanted to keep her as real, as substantial as the sharp elbows and bony heels she'd felt poking at her belly. So she gave her a name: Karen.

How does one go home to family dinners and algebra classes after such an experience? Joanne never really did. Quickly, she found a man to marry—and then divorce when he turned out to be alcoholic and abusive. A few years later she met and married Joe, an easygoing army sergeant from Montana who firmly believed that "family's the only thing you've got." She knew how much Joe loved her when she told him about Karen. "It's a damn shame," he reassured her. "If we'd met sooner, I sure would have raised that girl as my own." His unwavering acceptance cut through her shame.

A few years later, when Joe was stationed in Germany, they decided to adopt two baby girls just ten months apart, Monika and Gail (who now goes by Gerlinde). The couple so far had been unable to conceive. But her daughters speculate that Joanne also may have wanted to atone for the baby she had given up. When the German babies were barely two, Joanne got a surprise: She became pregnant again, with a daughter, Laurie, who all agree was always special to Joanne. Over the next few years two more girls came along, Jennie and Judy. Of the two fair-haired girls she'd adopted and the three dark-eyed, olive-skinned ones she had by Joe, none looked much like Joanne.

The family eventually settled in Whittier, California, near Joe's tight-knit extended family. He got a job tending the county pound, and "the Boss," as Joe called Joanne, stayed home with the girls. She had an artist's touch, and in her spare time drew or painted, knitted afghans or sewed quilts. "It was maybe not as wholesome as Beaver Cleaver's life, but I couldn't have asked for a better childhood," Jennie says. There wasn't a lot of money. But, Jennie says, "we always got love."

Outside the family, Joanne never talked about the child she gave up. But within their close circle, the story was well-known. She told all the girls about their missing sister. Decades later, she'd still say to Joe, "I wonder what she's like. I wonder if she's married or if she had kids."

Even as the memory lost its painful edge, an aftertaste of sadness hung on. "I think her whole life, she was trying to fill a void," her daughter Monika says. Maybe that's why, she adds, at age 65, Joanne insisted the family leave California—where she and Joe had lived for 40 years—and move to Idaho to be near the brother with whom she'd never been close. "It's like she kept looking for something." And soon enough, that something—a nervous Mary Anne Duffy—was knocking on her door.

Bonding with Strangers

Some researchers believe we are driven to search out and favor biological kin. People tend to hunt much harder for a lost parent or sibling than for a missing cousin, points out Nancy L. Segal, a developmental psychologist at California State University in Fullerton. "It appears we have an evolutionary predisposition to be more altruistic to someone with whom we share genes," she says. "It's a way to preserve the genetic pool."

Segal has studied twins who were separated soon after birth, reared in different families, and reunited as adults. In her book *Entwined Lives: Twins and What They Tell Us About Human Behavior*, she describes one part of that research, in which she asked 122 people who'd been intuited with a twin to rate how tight a bond they felt when they first met. Most of the identical twins described very strong feelings of familiarity, saying that this stranger with whom they shared the same genetic blueprint felt more familiar than a best friend, and that they anticipated becoming as close as best friends.

"It feels almost counterintuitive that people might feel so close to someone they never knew," says Segal. "But it makes sense when you think about biological connectedness."

Flying out on the plane to Idaho, Mary Anne was impatient to meet her newfound family. But once she and Chuck checked into the roadside motel in Post Falls, she began stalling for time, unpacking the suitcases, carefully folding and putting away their clothes. Despite all she had learned about Joanne from their exchange of several letters and calls, she suddenly realized she didn't really know this woman at all. And what about Joanne's husband, Joe? Or the daughters—her sisters? "Here's this person they may have always known about. But knowing about me and having me physically show up was a whole new ball game," Mary Anne says. Would they like her? Would she like them?

Mary Anne's Family History

Then it happened, like a dream Mary Anne can still see in front of her. She and Chuck are pulling into the half-circle of gravel in front of her mother's house, a prefabricated home with a lovely garden and tall trees. And then a dark-haired woman named Jennie—her *sister* Jennie!—is standing in front of her, saying hello, leading into the house. And a balding man with basset hound eyes, Joe, shuffles up to give her a hug. And then there is Joanne, lurching out of her wheelchair to wrap her arms around her, though in truth she's so frail that it is Mary Anne who gingerly enfolds her.

"My God, you look like my mom!" Jennie exclaims, before reminding herself to drop the "my." Looking at Joanne's gaunt face, Mary Anne sees a faint echo of herself. But it's not until she looks at photos of a younger Joanne, with her wide lap, heavy arms, and robust farm-wife good looks, that she gasps, "That's me." After a lifetime, the mystery of her looks is solved. "At last," she laughs, "I know who to blame for my hips and thin hair."

They settle at the kitchen table—where Joanne has always held court—and start to talk. Joanne can't take her eyes off Mary Anne. She drinks her in with the thirst of a new mother for her baby. As one of the sisters, Laurie, later said, "She'd of counted her fingers and toes if she could."

All day long, and the next and the next, they sit at the oval table comparing notes. Her daughters Jennie and Laurie and Judy stay near to fill in the details Joanne can't recall. Mary Anne doesn't press too hard, afraid of hurting Joanne with painful memories. She's also careful about what she offers. She doesn't want to paint her childhood so grim that it stirs Joanne's guilt or so gilded that the Munozes feel outclassed.

Sometime during the visit, the family gives Mary Anne a manila folder they've filled with stacks of photos and family papers. She learns that one of Joanne's great-grandfathers fought for the Union Army and was a prisoner of war at Andersonville, Georgia. Gerlinde, the family genealogist, has traced Joanne's ancestry all the way back to the *Mayflower*. Mary Anne is staggered. In the time it takes to look through the papers, she is transformed from orchid to oak, from a singular flower feeding on air to a tree drawing sustenance from deep, old roots.

After she gets back to her suburban Chicago home, she buys a plastic loose-leaf binder to put together a genealogy book. Not the borrowed genealogy of the Replogles—she tossed that family tree years ago during a move. But her history: the photographs of Joanne and Joe and their daughters and grandchildren and Joanne's parents and grandparents and great-grandparents; even the daguerreotype of the Civil War veteran and Mary Anne's research on the battles in which he fought. She writes carefully on the spine "Mary Anne's family history" and sticks a Post-it in the front explaining whom the book is intended for: her daughter, Diana.

Family Ties

As Mary Anne and Joanne got to know one another, they and the sisters reveled in the eerie parallels. "Mary Anne was like Mom all over again," says Jennie. It wasn't just their looks, but also the way each had experienced the world. Both were close to their mothers and had difficult relations with their fathers. Both had married early and badly to get away from their dominating dads. Each had battled all her life with her weight and feelings of inferiority. Joanne, says Jennie, "was always chubby as a little girl, and she always felt Grandpa was disappointed in the way she looked, that she wasn't elegant like her mother."

They also shared many of the same tastes. Both loved classical music and Irish tenors. Both loved animals, though Joanne's passion was for cats and Mary Anne preferred dogs. Both were voracious readers with a special interest in history. Both liked steak and iced tea. Each had the same habit of sticking out her tongue at her husband when teased.

How much did sharing some of the same genes account for those similarities? Again, studies of separated twins provide some clues. University of Minnesota psychologist Thomas J. Bouchard Jr. has for 20 years exhaustively interviewed some 130 sets of such twins. Identical twins typically come within six or seven points of one another on IQ tests. Likewise on measures of what are considered core personality traits, such as whether someone is outgoing or shy, cooperative or quarrelsome, organized or disorderly, calm or unstable, imaginative or narrow-minded. Though it differs from person to person, says Bouchard, the evidence suggests that genes account for 40 to 50 percent of the variability seen in the characteristics that make us who we are. "It's not that your genes are making you do things one way or the other," he explains. "But people with the same genes have similar mechanisms in their brains. And so they can respond to things in their environment in the same way."

Studies by Bouchard and Segal have found that even twins raised under different circumstances can end up displaying startling similarities. In one celebrated case, twins who were reunited at age 39 discovered, among other things, that each had worked part-time as a sheriff, smoked Salem cigarettes, bit his fingernails, suffered migraines, given his son the same name, and liked to scatter love notes to his wife around the house.

Such coincidences are not only seen in reunited twins, Bouchard adds. "I've heard the same stories about daughters who found their mothers."

"She Just Belonged"

Over the next year and a half, Mary Anne returned three more times to see Joanne, while keeping close through weekly phone calls. Each visit deepened her connection to her family, and she found herself more at ease in their modest home than she ever was amid the finery that surrounded her growing up. "I'm much more comfortable in a jeans-and-sweatshirt environment," she says.

From the start, it was easy to call Joanne "Mom." "Once I got past the nervousness, my gut reaction was that I liked her. I enjoyed being with her," Mary Anne says. "I didn't feel I had to be somebody I wasn't. I was just me."

But family, Mary Anne found, is created by emotional connections, not just blood. For as close as she felt to Joanne, she also found a deep kinship with Joe. He accepted her without question, just as he had always told Joanne he would. He didn't give a hoot about her weight; if anything, Mary Anne's roundness was a comforting reminder of Joanne before she got so desperately ill. By the end of the first visit, she was calling him Papa Joe. And during her second visit, after she heard him casually tell a store clerk she was his daughter, she started calling him Dad. "The love he has shown and expressed for me is more love than I ever got from my father," says Mary Anne. "I just fell in love with him."

And there was an immediate rapport with her five sisters. For their part, the sisters say there was nothing forced about their willingness to welcome Mary Anne into the fold. "Maybe it was because we knew about her forever," Jennie explains. Then, too, they knew their mother's health was failing and how happy it made her to meet Mary Anne.

"It was easy to love her," says Laurie. "She just belonged." It helped that Mary Anne had the same easygoing style and bantering sense of humor. At Christmas, all the sisters made a point of traveling to Joanne's house, though the five Munoz girls hadn't been together in one place in more than ten years. Everyone laughed when the cameras came out, and Mary Anne jockeyed with her heavy-hipped sisters for the coveted spot behind Joanne's wheelchair that would hide them from the waist down.

A Sense of Fullness

She felt a strong bond with all the sisters. But with Monika and Gerlinde, Mary Anne also shared the adoption experience. While they may have grown up in a more loving family than Mary Anne's, they also sometimes felt that their family was not wholly their own. They were the two who acted out as teens, the ones who wound up living far from Joanne and Joe as adults.

"When Mary Anne and Monika and I had a chance to sit down and talk, we all came up with the same story," says Gerlinde. She'd also gone in search of her roots. But in her case, the birth mother never told anyone about Gerlinde. So while the reunion was sweet, it was also uncomfortable, and the two are only rarely in touch. It was Gerlinde who calmed Joanne's fears when Joanne first heard from Mary Anne. "She said, 'What do you think she wants?'" Gerlinde recalls. "And I said, 'She just wants to know you, her mother.'"

As Mary Anne was drawn into the family, she was transformed. Before, she was so reserved that she told hardly anyone when she got married. Now, instead of waiting to bump into friends to tell them about the reunion, she eagerly phoned to share the news. In the past, she'd greet her old friend Kris Ronnow at church with a handshake. Now she offered warm hugs. "It's like she came alive," says Ronnow.

She also started eating differently, and not by following some faddish diet or obsessively counting calories, which had always failed her. She simply cut back on what she put in her mouth and avoided the fries and pastries and ice cream that had always eroded her self-control.

At first she was pleasantly baffled by this newfound ability to push away the plate when she was full. Then she realized—how trite but true!—that the emptiness she'd tried vainly to stuff with food had disappeared. Over the next year she dropped from 280 pounds to 170, barely trying. "I felt complete," she explains.

So did Joanne. Sometimes at night she'd say to Joe, "I'm so happy I got to meet Mary Anne."

Good-Bye to "Mom"

We usually think of family, at least parents and siblings, as people we have no choice about. But sometimes, if we're lucky, they might also be people whom we choose to know and love. After more than 50 years, the chosen child finally got to make that choice. She still keeps in touch with her sister Betsy and is close with her Replogle cousins. But on her desk at home, it's a portrait of Joe and Joanne that she sets in the place of honor. She'll always feel tenderness for Mary, but it's Joanne she now refers to when she says "Mom." And in place of the father she never knew, or the one she knew but who couldn't give her what she needed, she has the father she always wanted: Joe.

In June 1999, a little more than a year after the initial visit, Mary Anne and Chuck made one more trip to see Joanne. While they were there, Joanne complained that she didn't feel well. When they took her to the doctor, he diagnosed pneumonia and admitted her to the hospital. After a few days, she seemed much better. On their way to the airport, Mary Anne and Chuck stopped by the hospital to say good-bye. Mary Anne sat on her mother's bed, and they talked about Joanne coming to Chicago in the fall. The two would revisit all the old haunts—their childhood homes, their high schools, the hospital where both were born. Together they'd call up the old ghosts and chase them away.

Then it was time to leave. I love you, Mary Anne said, kissing her mother on the cheek. I love you, too, Joanne answered. They threw each other one more kiss. Eight days later, Joanne died.

Most of the family was too distraught to deal with the arrangements, so Mary Anne helped Jennie and Judy plan the funeral. They all knew that Joanne had loved the traditional Irish Blessing and suggested that Chuck read it.

"May the road rise up to meet you, may the wind be always at your back . . . And until we meet again . . ." He was doing fine until he looked up and saw Mary Anne crying with the rest of her family.

Adopting the Children of a Deceased Relative

Nancy Hanner

In the following selection, Nancy Hanner tells of her unplanned route to adoptive parenthood. In 1992 Hanner became the legal guardian to the young children of her deceased relatives. After contending with the early difficulties of caring for her niece and nephew, Hanner, with her husband's consent, decided to adopt the children. Hanner concludes that though the trials have been great, she is glad of the experience and grateful for her untraditional family. Hanner lives in Lexington, Kentucky.

Eleven years ago, I arrived at the funeral of my brother-in-law as both a mourning relative and the sudden legal guardian of his two children. It was the family's second funeral in the course of a year. Nine months earlier, my sister-in-law, niece and nephew had died in a tragic accident. People approached me, pressed my hands and said, "You are so wonderful to take these children."

It was a noble view of adoption, with me the rescuer, the saver of children. It was tempting to buy into it, and I did at times. But once I got down to the business of raising children, I found that that perspective had little to do with the reality of creating a family.

After the funeral, my husband and I moved into my brother-in-law's house so we wouldn't further disrupt the lives of our new 18-month-old son and 2-year-old daughter. Those first three months were so stressful I developed a case of hives that I couldn't shake. The hives eventually went away, but it took a lot longer to work through the emotional problems. Despite my best efforts at forging a relationship with her, my daughter gave me the cold shoulder for the first five years she was with us. Her favorite story was "Cinderella," and I'm fairly certain I wasn't the Fairy Godmother.

Second Choice Mother

I have a friend who became a full-time stepmother one weekend when her husband's ex-wife decided she could no longer care for the children. She raised the kids, monitoring late-night asthma attacks, baking room-mother treats and sitting through Scout meetings.

"My daughter invited me to the mother's weekend at college," she told me one day. "Then she found out her real mother could make it, so she called back to uninvite me."

I was shocked at her daughter's heartless treatment of the mother who had always been there for her. My friend and I are No. 2—we will never truly be No. 1 in our kids' eyes, and that is one of the not-so-nice realities of adoption.

We are quick to point out what we consider our children's misdirected loyalties, but what of our own? My friend's preference would have been to have raised a traditional family with her husband. Mine was also to have children of my own, which I attempted to do without success for seven years. However much we pretend otherwise, our adopted children were second choices for us.

So there it is. Our children want what they have lost, and so do we. They have lost their blood ties to parents. We have lost our visions of family, the dream of how our lives should look.

I recently read about a family who brought a baby girl back from China. The whole family passionately wanted to do this. The oldest son comes home from college more often now so he can play with her. The kids developed a schedule because they all wanted to hold her at the same time. This family adopted their daughter for the purest of reasons: they had love to give, and felt compelled to offer it. That's all. So many people don't start in the right place as this family did, but those who are willing to work through the disillusionment that follows have a chance to grow into a real family unit.

Simply Family

A few months ago my 12-year-old daughter called from her grandmother's house, where she was visiting for the week. She has a special bond with this grandmother, the mother of the mother she lost. "I miss the dog," she said, then laughed. "Oh, and I miss you, too." When I hung up, I was glad for all those years that we moved slowly together, circling each other—afraid to place our vulnerability in each other's hands. She did miss me. I could hear it in her voice.

My son is now old enough to understand chromosomes and the steps beyond the mechanics of reproduction. My husband's blood runs through my son, but mine does not, and he knows it. "There is a ceremony," I told him, thinking this would appeal greatly to an 11-year-old boy, "where we can become blood brothers. We can do it if you want." He considered it and said no, I imagine because of the part involving blood. Now I wonder if it was I who wanted the ceremony, if I was still longing for the solidity of a blood bond.

I feel ridiculous for having suggested this idea, realizing he has no need for such things—that he is, in fact, exactly where he should be. He knows where his family is, both the one that is buried and the one that sits at the hockey rink, watching him play. And because he is such a great kid, he is willing to be patient with a mother who sometimes likes to make her mission much more complicated than what it really is: the offering of family, simple, sweet and pure.

Contrasting Experiences of Reunions with Birth Mothers

Sarah Saffian

In the following selection from *Cosmopolitan*, writer Sarah Saffian presents the stories of two young women whose experiences meeting their birth mothers ended very differently. Sonia Lloyd bounced from an abusive adoptive family to foster care before being sought out by her own birth mother. At the time Sonia was only sixteen, but her meeting with her birth mother proved life-changing. She instantly formed a strong relationship with her birth mother and spent the remainder of her childhood with her. Katherine Greene grew up happily in her adoptive home, but when faced with the idea of starting a family of her own, she felt the need to learn more about her birth parents and her own past. To her birth mother, Katherine represented a painful reminder of a past event, and the two did not remain in contact. Saffian is a journalist and author of *Ithaka: A Daughter's Memoir of Being Found.*

Editor's Note: All names have been changed to protect the privacy of the individuals.

My earliest memory is from when I was 5. My mother, younger sister, and I were walking down the street. (My mother had three kids after she adopted me.) A lady strode up, looked at me, and said, "What a beautiful girl." I grinned, but as the lady walked away, my mother snapped, "Wipe that smile off your face! You're not cute." Later, I realized she was angry because the lady had ignored her "real" daughter.

Growing up, my mom always favored my younger siblings and said I was the "bad seed." For punishment, she once took off my clothes, taped my hands behind my back, and spanked me with an extension cord. My dad would just turn a blind eye, so like many abused kids, I internalized the situation and became convinced I would never amount to anything.

When I was 13, I was putting laundry away in my father's drawer and found a binder of documents. I opened it and saw adoption papers with my birth date on them. All of a sudden, it made sense why I had been treated so badly. I was scared to say anything to my parents, but I told the school counselor, who said she'd call them and they'd probably talk with me about it. But my parents didn't bring it up until one Sunday in the car, when my mother turned to my father and said, "By the way, Sonia knows she's adopted." And my sister squealed, "Ooh, that means *I'm* really the oldest!"

At first, I was totally devastated by my discovery, but soon it became empowering. "At least I'm not one of *them*," I could tell myself. My parents reacted to my new attitude by coming down on me even harder. My dad started disciplining me by hitting me with his belt, and my mom began locking me out of the house. One afternoon, I came home from school and she called out the window. "You stay outside till your father gets here." It was the middle of February and cold, so I went to a friend's house, where I frequently took refuge. When I came back a few hours later, my father yanked me inside by the collar and started hitting me. I managed to get away from him and ran back to my friend's house. Her mom started crying and said, "I'm sick of watching this happen. I'm calling the police." When I was assigned to a social worker and placed in a foster family, I was really relieved. The family court wanted me to go back home, but I was determined not to and my social worker supported me. I saw a psychiatrist with my parents a few times but never went to live with them again.

A Fateful Phone Call

At the foster home, there was no structure, no guidance at all—15 to 20 people aged infant to adult stayed there every night. By 16, I lost all motivation and dropped out of high school. I got a job at Burger King and spent most nights at my boyfriend's house. Then one day, one of my foster sisters knocked on my boyfriend's door. "Your mom called," she said. I thought she meant my adoptive mom, and I said I didn't want to talk to her. "No, your *mother* called." As we drove back to the foster home, I was in a daze. Someone handed me the phone number, and I started to cry hysterically. Someone else dialed the number my birth mother, Jane Miner, left. When she answered, my first words to her were "Please come get me."

Jane, who is white, explained that when she was 18, she'd gotten pregnant with me, by her boyfriend, who was black. She had given me up because her parents would not let her raise a half-black baby in their house. Two years later, she and the same boyfriend had a son named Sam, who is my full biological brother. But after he was born, she found out my birth father was cheating on her, so she broke up with him and raised Sam by herself. She'd started looking for me a few months earlier, after joining a birth-mother support group that put her in touch with a professional searcher. When she learned that I had been put in foster care, she felt horrible. During our phone call, she asked what had happened, and I told her everything.

A month after that first conversation, Jane and Sam came, like saviors, to rescue me. I met them at the airport, and the three of us stood in one another's arms, sobbing, for a good 15 minutes. I felt so much love and nurturing from Jane that I started calling her Mom right away. Over the next few days, I introduced Jane and Sam to my foster family and showed them where my adoptive family lived, but they didn't meet. Then at the end of the visit, I got on the plane with them to go back to Los Angeles. I didn't even tell my foster family. I just left.

Once we were in California, Jane contacted my caseworker, who said she had to return me to my foster family. But instead, Jane enrolled me in Sam's high school and hired a lawyer, and a few months later, she was granted foster rights. At first, I wanted so badly to be mothered that I was like a wounded puppy, eyes down, unable to speak. But Jane and I talked a lot about her giving me up, and eventually, I was able to express my anger about it. Over time, we came to understand each other's experiences and grew very close. She's an extremely warmhearted woman—an excellent listener and a loving caretaker.

I graduated from high school on time and served in the Army for eight years, the last three at Fort Meade, Maryland. Then I enrolled in college there and graduated with associate degrees in accounting and management. For the past three years, I've worked for the Department of Defense. Even though Jane still lives in Los Angeles, we're now as close as if she'd raised me all along. We see each other a few times a year and talk and E-mail constantly. Last Christmas, she came to visit me for three weeks, and if she's anywhere within 300 miles, I'll go meet her. But no matter where we are, we both know how much we're loved and supported by each other, and that's a wonderful feeling.

Katherine's Story

I grew up near Harrisburg, Pennsylvania, with my brother, Robert, who is four years younger and also adopted. My childhood was very happy, and my parents took great care of us. On weekends, our dad would take us on day trips. Our house was like a playground—lots of friends would come over to work on arts-and-crafts projects our mom gave us or to play spy games in the clubhouse Dad built in the backyard.

But as I grew older, I realized that one day, I would want to search for my birth parents. As a teenager, I faced so many questions about my own identity: *Who did I look and act like? Where did my artistic talent come from?* At the same time, it seemed better to wait until I was away from home and had some distance to begin actually searching. Years passed. When I was a senior in college, I began dating a classmate, Andrew. After we graduated in 1999, we moved in together. We were talking about marriage, and I started wondering what I would tell my children about my birth parents and what my health history was. *I'm an adult, and I don't know a thing about myself,* I thought. It was time to start looking for answers.

My parents were supportive but had limited information about my birth mother—brown hair, brown eyes, average build. They knew her name, Jessie Nelson, because the lawyer who had handled the adoption let it slip. I did research and learned I could request my adoption records from the county courthouse for $50. Annoyed that I had to pay for my own information, I called my mom and vented to her about the whole process. The next day, she E-mailed me at work and dropped a bombshell: "You're so determined to know the truth. I've been trying to find a way to tell you this," she began. "Your birth mother told the adoption lawyer she was raped." In shock, I told my coworkers I was sick and went home. It felt creepy to share DNA with someone capable of such violence. And I felt betrayed that my parents had kept this fact from me for so long. They said they'd been scared of hurting me, but my mom decided finally to tell me because she didn't want me to have to find out from someone else.

Suddenly, I wasn't sure if I wanted to find my birth mother, mostly because I was worried she wouldn't want to meet me. But I decided to keep searching, thinking any truth was better than not knowing at all. I also held out hope that the information about the rape had been wrong. I received the courthouse documents, which said that Jessie was 26 when she gave me up and that she was born in West Virginia where, I learned, all birth records are at the library and open to the public. In March 2001, I traveled from my home in Allentown, Pennsylvania, to Charleston, West Virginia, found Jessie in the index, and got her birth certificate from the Vital Registration Office. When I came home, I plugged her information into a search Web site and found her current address and phone number in Clearwater, Florida.

A Traumatic Reunion

I waited until the weekend to call because I wanted to be alone. As I dialed her number, I was shaking so much that I could barely hold the phone. But an answering machine picked up, giving no name, and I didn't want to leave a message. I kept trying, but after a week of not reaching her, I looked up the phone number of her mother, who lived in Morgantown, West Virginia, and called. By sheer coincidence, Jessie happened to be visiting, and her mother passed the phone to her. "I have something sensitive to talk to you about," I said. "I'm an adoptee looking for my birth mother, and I think she might be you." Silence. Then, "Well, this is very strange!" She said she'd be home in a couple of weeks and we could talk then.

In the meantime, I decided to write her a letter. I thought it would be easier for me to express myself and easier for her to digest. I thanked her and assured her I had a good life and good parents and wasn't looking for another mother. "I know the circumstances of my birth, so if you don't want to see me, I understand," I wrote. "But I'd like to meet, if you want to." From her reply, I could tell Jessie was conflicted. "It's not a question of what I want," she responded. "I feel like I'm a match for somebody who needs a kidney. Do I want to donate a kidney? No. Do I want to be the kind of person to say no? No."

Crushed, I showed my parents her letter. My mom was angry at Jessie and protective of me but also admitted that if she were me, she'd want to meet her birth mother too. So that August, I flew to Florida to meet Jessie. I stayed in a hotel, but we spent much of the weekend together. We walked on the beach and talked, then went back to her house and looked through her photo albums and had dinner with her boyfriend. She said lots of nice things, such as "I have no regrets. You're intelligent and beautiful, and there's no reason on earth that you can't meet life's challenges."

But by the second day, I could sense her pulling back. At one point, I asked if she in fact had been raped and if she had known my father. She shuddered and said, "What good will it do you to know?" I said I needed the truth. Yes, she replied, it had been a rape, and he'd been an acquaintance but not a romantic interest. I wanted to ask his name but didn't have the heart to keep going. Then later that night, she said out of the blue, "This is the only time we'll see each other." I felt paralyzed. I'd tried to prepare myself for the possibility of rejection, but I thought things had been going well. "Can I still write to you?" I managed to choke out, and after hesitation, she nodded her head yes. The next day, as we said good-bye in the hotel lobby, she told me how glad she was that she had brought me into the world. She paused, then said, "I'm going to get up and walk away now." Watching her leave was the hardest thing I've ever had to do.

Back in the Family Fold

After our reunion, I wrote Jessie that I was happy to have met her and hoped we could keep corresponding. She wrote back and basically told me to get over it and move on. At first I was hurt, but I've come to understand that her actions are not about who I am but about her difficulty dealing with what happened to her. After the rape, she never married and never had other children. I think that facing me was like facing her rapist all over again and the reality of an experience she denied all these years and that was just too painful for her.

Now that I've finally learned about Jessie, I've been able to shift my focus. In June, Andrew and I got married. The wedding was outdoors at a bed-and-breakfast near our home. We had perfect weather, and I felt so close to everyone—my family, my friends, my new husband. My mother helped me with my veil, and my father walked me down the aisle. "Wow!" I remember thinking at the time. "I have so much love in my life!"

SINGLE-PARENT ADOPTIVE FAMILIES WORK

Nancy E. Dowd

In the following article, Nancy E. Dowd tells the story of the path she took to become an adoptive single parent. Single parents who adopt have unique obstacles to overcome, Dowd says. They must first convince themselves that a single-parent environment can be good for a child; they have fewer options than do married couples trying to adopt; and they face greater scrutiny from social workers who must approve potential adoptive parents through a home study process. But once the adoption is complete, single-parent adoptive families have a high likelihood of functioning well, Dowd says, because of the deliberate way in which the single-parent family was formed. Dowd is a law professor at the University of Florida Levin College of Law.

I never dreamed that I would adopt two children on my own. The two-parent heterosexual married model of parenthood was firmly inscribed on my consciousness at a young age, and the certainty that life would unfold this way was unshakeable. But in my late thirties, divorced, childless but still strongly desiring children, I began the process that ultimately would lead to the adoption of my daughter when I was just past my fortieth birthday, followed by the adoption of my son three years later.

> "So does that mean you're an unwed mother?"
> —a friend, in response to my first adoption

Probably the most difficult process for most single people who adopt is valuing and validating their decision. Choosing to create a family on one's own seems somehow selfish, although adopting a child sounds somehow more sacrificing than selfish. Nevertheless, creating a single-parent family, rather than such a family occurring as a result of divorce, death, or never marrying, is a highly disfavored social choice. Single-parent families are loaded with societal stigma, and therefore a decision to voluntarily create one seems anomalous. On the other hand, the very commonality of single-parent families also makes the creation of such a family less remarkable and more acceptable. Two-thirds of children will spend some time before the age of eighteen in a single-parent family. A child raised by a single parent is hardly uncommon and would not be subject to special scrutiny. More important, the stigma attached to this form of family is unsupported by the data on single-parent families. It is function rather than form that matters; what families do, rather than what they look like.

> "Because there are so many single-parent homes, your children won't stand out, won't feel so different."
>
> —my social worker, during the home study in my first adoption

For me, then, as for other single parents, the critical first step is imagining this choice as one that is good for a child. The second step is determining whether it can be done. Up until fairly recently, the answer would have been no; only married couples were eligible to adopt. But in 1988, when I began the process leading to my first adoption, I discovered that many routes were available for single people to adopt: domestic and international programs, as well as a range within each of those options. The sheer number of options is certainly not close to that available to married couples, but in many respects that makes the process of sorting out options easier, since you are not so overwhelmed.

I ultimately decided to do an independent adoption, meaning that I would connect with the child that I would adopt through an intermediary.

Intense Scrutiny

Regardless of legal entitlement to adopt, it is social workers and lawyers who control the adoption process, and without their support, individuals can rarely be successful in pushing against this informal bureaucratic structure. It is critical for single parents to work with a program and people who support single-parent adoption. Even with that assurance, I was sensitive to the scrutiny of me not only as an adoptive parent, but as a single adoptive parent, during the home study process. It seemed essential to establish that I had thought through the consequences of parenting a child alone, what strategies I would use for the benefit of the child and myself. Providing role models of the missing gender (in my case a male) was clearly important. Assuring the presence of help and support was also critical, because of the stress of parenting alone. The home study process can be excruciating, because you have no clear sense of exactly what the social worker is looking for, only that this person holds the key to whether you will be able to adopt. I simply saw the outcome as fated (or not), and just followed the process rather than fighting the intrusion. Ultimately, my social worker and I worked as a team rather than as adversaries.

But a critical factor in my adoption was that I am female. Single-parent male adoption is much less common than single-parent female adoption. A woman raising a child on her own seems unremarkable, reflecting common patterns of single parenthood for nonmarital couples and divorced couples. Mothers more commonly are caregivers; fathers more commonly are secondary parents, economic parents, or absent parents. Men's parenting is strongly mediated by women, particularly the presence of women in their household. Men presenting themselves as single parents, then, are likely to face more intense explicit or implicit scrutiny.

The gender issues also relate to issues of sexual orientation and sexuality. Single-parent adoptions implicitly operate on a model of presumed heterosexuality, yet sexually active single parents or cohabiting single parents are less desirable, since the role of the boyfriend or cohabiting partner is unclear and might be deemed a destabilizing factor and therefore not in the best interests of the child for placement. The question of sexual orientation may be explicit or implicit, and the consequence of revelation of gay or lesbian status may also imperil adoption unless the program and persons running the program support the adoption of children by single parents whether gay or lesbian, and by gays and lesbians whether single or in committed relationships.

In the course of my home study this issue came up in questions regarding my life preceding the home study, which included the fact that I had been married and divorced, and the question of whether I had thought about the consequences of adopting for my future social life and likelihood of marrying again. Because I fit the heterosexual norm, but was not engaged in a significant relationship at the time, I was safe and sexless at the point of adoption.

Adoptive Parent "Marketing"

Once I was approved at the end of the home study process, the real process of connecting with my daughter began. In many forms of adoption this stage requires that you provide information about yourself to the program or to an intermediary, and again, a single person may feel a sense of needing to justify themselves, to construct themselves so that they are a good choice for placement. Because birth parents increasingly have an active or exclusive role in deciding where their child will be placed, one tries to imagine how placing a child with just one parent would seem to be a good choice. Probably the most important reassurance, however, is that everyone that I have known, single or married, who has begun and stayed with the adoption process has been successful. Even if the fears are real, they are offset by the realities of the numbers of placements with single parents.

I had decided to work with a lawyer well known for her expertise in placing children. After laboring over a letter describing myself to potential birth mothers or birth parents and sending my best picture of myself to go along with the letter, I was surprised to get a critique back from the lawyer's assistant. They suggested changes in the letter and ways I might have a picture taken, all designed to make me more desirable as a choice of a parent. This marketing aspect was very uncomfortable for me. Indeed, despite the effort to distinguish adoption from baby selling, the reality is that it feels very much like a marketplace.

There was something about the process of choosing, rather like ordering a child, that uncomfortably feels like baby selling or seeing children as property. Race is as omnipresent as money in adoption. Health factors are also present; there is a strong presumption of the desirability of a "perfect" child with no "defects" or disabilities, major or minor. And in some programs, gender is also an acceptable preference factor. Finally, I had to decide about the process of advertising and where in the country to advertise. Did I want the birth mother or birth parents to be located far away from me? Did I want them to come from a rural or urban area? What states? The questions forced me to think about my ideal birth parents as well as my concept of connection or contact with the birth parents after the adoption.

Finding a Child, Meeting the Birth Mother

Finally I was ready to try to connect with a child. It had taken me nearly two years to get to this point. When anyone asks me about adoption, my first question is how old are you. Your age, more than anything, affects your attractiveness as an adoptive parent. It also affects how long you have to decide whether adoption might work for you, gather information, and work through the process to the point where you stand ready and available to begin the legal process of adoption. For a single parent, the time factor may be even stronger, although in the programs that work with single parents, it seems that the time factor from readiness to adopt to completion of an adoption is no longer than for married couples. Particularly because the age at which people have their first child is increasing, together with the time taken trying to become pregnant and deal with infertility, most people come to adoption in their thirties. Rarely do parents come to adoption first.

When I was ready, it was not through my chosen, well-calculated, studied, and researched path that my daughter came to me. My best friend from law school encouraged me to talk to one of her law firm partners, who had adopted three children. He put me in contact with both intermediaries, one a social worker, one a lawyer. Two months later, ten days before Christmas, the lawyer called me at work and told me that she had a baby for me, if I was willing. My heart stopped, just about. The baby was due in May or early June, and was the child of two teenagers. The parents had asked the lawyer to decide where to place the child. This lawyer had chosen me. It is a mystery and a blessing that I will never forget.

I arrived in Phoenix, where my daughter was born, five days before she was due. She was born seven days later. Waiting. Waiting. I felt like I held my breath, just waiting for her to come into being. A few days after I got to Phoenix, and before she was born, the lawyer called.

"The birth mom knows you are in town and would like to meet you. Would you be willing to meet her?"

Of course I would meet with her. But as I prepared for that meeting, I was intensely aware that the balance of power was completely out of my hands. Indeed, this is the reality of independent adoption—the parent or parents can change their mind, since no legally enforceable commitment can be made prior to birth. Yet on the other side of adoption is an equally lopsided balance of power, totally on the side of the adoptive parents. Promises of contact and information and ongoing connection are generally not legally enforceable, only morally obligating. But what began in that meeting has continued to this day—an extraordinary connection and ongoing communication that has been one of the most amazing aspects of this whole amazing process. It defies every stereotype of adoption, the mythology of conflict between birth parents and adoptive parents, the rationale for secrecy, and the fear still generated for every adoptive parent that someday the "real" parents will reappear and somehow dissolve the bonds between them and their children.

Life as a Single Adoptive Parent

Life as a single adoptive parent is no more difficult than it is for any single parent, or perhaps less so. Since single adoptive parents have chosen parenthood in this form, the financial aspects of single parenting are more likely not to be the challenge that single adoptive parents typically face. The most significant challenge faced by most single-mother families are economic challenges, in addition to the social stigma placed on single-parent families. The most significant challenge faced by single fathers, on the other hand, is the lack of social and cultural support for nurturing fatherhood, as well as the lack of economic structures to support fathers as nurturers rather than as breadwinners. Single-parent families nevertheless are commonplace, and that social reality makes single parenting of adoptive children easier, for both parents and children. The parents have access to the expertise of other single parents. The children do not stand out as unique or different in a world with a range of family forms.

None of this is to suggest that adoptees do not face developmental issues that are not faced by biological children raised by their biological parents. Those issues are clearly present, particularly in a world that is suffused with mythology about adoption and identity. But those issues are not significantly different for single adoptive parents as compared to couples who adopt.

The challenges facing single adoptive fathers parallel those of all single fathers, who remain in a distinct minority of all single parents who are primary caregivers. Similarly, the challenges facing gay and lesbian single parents relate to social and community acceptance and support, similar to biological parents.

The most important lesson from the data on single-parent families is that family success and good outcomes for children do not depend on form, but on function. Single-parent families can function as successfully as dual-parent families. They function similarly in the bottom line provision of care, and differently in that the structure affects how they carry out their function. But they are not second-class families any more than adopted children are second-class children. Single-parent families work, and single-parent adoptive families have a higher likelihood of functioning well because they are chosen families that lack the stress factors more common in single-parent families formed by non-marriage or divorce.

"Why Didn't You Have Your Own Children?"

Life for a single adoptive parent is also not significantly different from that of couples who adopt. The biological preference is strong for both. The open acknowledgment that my children are adopted always seems to lead to the question of why I didn't simply go get pregnant. Funny how the high school anathema turns into the flip solution to a single person's childlessness. Just as couples are asked about their infertility problems, single adoptive parents are often presumed fertile and questioned for their choice of adoption over biological parenthood. Children of single adoptive parents may find that their status as adoptees comes up more frequently than is the case for children placed with couples, who may be presumed biological children and therefore have the choice of whether to be open about their adoptive status.

The diversity of family forms makes my children feel relatively unremarkable. But there is no doubt that being adopted is different, and being adopted by a single parent is different. Not worse or better, just different. Parenting alone is not for everyone, but for those who take it on with full openness to the challenges, the rewards are amazing. As all parents know, children are the challenge, and the ultimate blessing, of a lifetime. Adoption magnifies that blessing, because your children come to you through the choices and sacrifices of others who rely on you to positively support their role in your children's lives.

Organizations to Contact

Abolish Adoption
PO Box 401, Palm Desert, CA 92261
e-mail: info@abolishadoption.com • Web site: www.abolishadoption.com

Abolish Adoption is an organization that petitions to end the practice of adoption. It believes that adoption is not in a child's best interests and violates human rights. Abolish Adoption also campaigns for open adoption record laws. Abolish Adoption sponsors and sells *The Ultimate Search Book: Worldwide Adoption, Genealogy & Other Search Secrets* by Lori Carangelo.

Adopting.com
e-mail: adopt@adopting.com • Web site: www.adopting.com

Adopting.com is a resource Web site offering a wealth of information that is useful for prospective adopters. Included on the site are links to several national adoption agencies, lawyers, letters to birth parents, and photo-listings of children who are up for adoption.

Adoption.com
e-mail: comments@adoption.com • Web site: http://adoption.com

Adoption.com is a Web-based network of adoption organizations. This collective site features profiles of prospective adoptive parents and adoptable children. It also posts articles that address adoption issues such as unplanned pregnancy, international adoption, and adoption reunions. Several publications and magazines, such as *2001 Adoption Guide* and *Adoption Today* magazine, are offered at this site.

Adoptive Families of America (AFA)
e-mail: letters@adoptivefamilies.com • Web site: www.adoptivefamilies.com

AFA serves as an umbrella organization supporting adoptive parents groups. It provides problem-solving assistance and information about the challenges of adoption to members of adoptive and prospective adoptive families. It also seeks to create opportunities for successful adoptive placement and promotes the health and welfare of children without permanent homes. AFA publishes the bimonthly magazine *Adoptive Families* (formerly *Ours* magazine).

American Adoption Congress (AAC)
PO Box 42730, Washington, DC 20015
(202) 483-3399
e-mail: patdenn@primenet.com
Web site: www.americanadoptioncongress.org

AAC is an educational network that promotes openness and honesty in adoption. It advocates adoption reform, including the opening of adoption records, and seeks to develop plans for alternative models for adoption. It directs attention to the needs of adult adoptees who are searching for their birth families. AAC publishes the quarterly *Search/Support Group Directory*.

Association for Research in International Adoption
University of South Alabama College of Nursing, Community Mental Health, Springhill Area Campus, Mobile, AL 36688-0002
(251) 434-3448 • fax: (251) 434-3995

e-mail: info@adoption-research.org • Web site: www.adoption-research.org

The ARIA Web site, maintained by the University of South Alabama College of Nursing, is an online clearinghouse for research relevant to the international adoption community. The site also contains links for adoptive parents wishing to learn more about the issues involved in adopting a foreign child.

Bastard Nation (BN)
PO Box 271672, Houston, TX 77277-1672
(415) 704-3166
e-mail: members@bastards.org • Web site: www.bastards.org

Bastard Nation is an adoptees' rights organization that campaigns to legalize adopted adults' access to records that pertain to their historical, genetic, and legal identities. It publishes a newsletter called *Bastard Quarterly*.

Child Welfare League of America (CWLA)
440 First St. NW, Suite 310, Third Floor, Washington, DC 20001
(202) 638-2952 • fax: (202) 638-4004
Web site: www.cwla.org

CWLA, a social welfare organization concerned with setting standards for welfare and human services agencies, encourages research on all aspects of adoption. It publishes *Child Welfare: A Journal of Policy, Practice, and Program.*

Concerned United Birthparents (CUB)
PO Box 503475, San Diego, CA 92150-3475
(800) 822-2777 • fax: (858) 435-4863
e-mail: info@CUBirthparents.org • Web site: www.cubirthparents.org

CUB provides assistance to birth parents, works to open adoption records, and seeks to develop alternatives to the current adoption system. It helps women considering the placement of a child for adoption to make an informed choice and seeks to prevent unnecessary separation of families by adoption. CUB publishes the monthly *Concerned United Birthparents-Communication.*

Dave Thomas Foundation for Adoption
4150 Tuller Rd. Suite 204, Dublin, Ohio 43017
(800) 275-3832 • fax: (614) 766-3871
e-mail: adoption@wendys.com
Web site: www.davethomasfoundationforadoption.org

The Dave Thomas Foundation for Adoption is a nonprofit public charity dedicated to increasing North American adoptions of children in foster care. Created by Dave Thomas, founder of Wendy's International, the foundation strives to raise awareness, share knowledge, and promote adoption through offering free resources and informational links to individuals and professional organizations with an interest in adoption. The foundation also offers grants to nonprofit organizations supporting adoption efforts.

Evan B. Donaldson Adoption Institute
525 Broadway, Sixth Floor, New York, NY 10012
(212) 925-4089 • fax: (775) 796-6592
e-mail: info@adoptioninstitue.org • Web site: www.adoptioninstitute.org

The Evan B. Donaldson Adoption Institute works with lawmakers, the media, adoption professionals, and public education services to make the issue of adoption more visible. The institute also publishes a series of books dealing with the ethics of adoption.

Families for Private Adoption (FPA)
PO Box 6375, Washington, DC 20015
(202) 722-0338
e-mail: ffpa@email.com • Web site: www.ffpa.org

FPA assists people considering private adoption (adoption without the use of an adoption agency). In addition to providing information on adoption procedures and legal concerns, it offers referrals to doctors, lawyers, and social workers. FPA publishes the quarterly *FPA Bulletin*.

Families Like Ours, Inc. (FLO)
PO Box 3137, Renton, WA 98056
(206) 441-7602 • fax: (425) 671-0856
Web site: www.familieslikeours.org

While FLO has an emphasis on gay and lesbian adoptive families, the non-profit organization also provides adoption resources and support to all families experiencing or investigating adoption. Their Web site offers articles, chat rooms, blogs, and links to additional resources.

Joint Council on International Children's Services (JCICS)
117 S. Saint Asaph St., Alexandria, VA 22314
(703) 535-8045 • fax: (703) 535-8049
e-mail: jcics@jcics.org • Web site: www.jcics.org

JCICS serves as an advocate on behalf of children needing permanent homes with caring families and promotes ethical practices in international adoption. Their Web site includes regularly updated links to the most recent information about adoption policies in the United States and many other countries around the world.

National Adoption Center (NAC)
1500 Walnut St., Suite 701, Philadelphia, PA 19102
(215) 735-9988
e-mail: nac@adopt.org • Web site: www.adopt.org

NAC promotes the adoption of older, disabled, and minority children and of siblings who seek to be placed together. It provides information, registration, family recruitment, and matching referral services for children and prospective adoptive parents. It publishes the semiannual *National Adoption Center Newsletter*.

National Adoption Information Clearinghouse (NAIC)
330 C St. SW, Washington, DC 20447
(888) 251-0075 or (703) 352-3488 • fax: (703) 385-3206
e-mail: naic@caliber.com • Web site: http://naic.acf.hhs.gov

The National Adoption Information Clearinghouse is a service provided by the U.S. Department of Health and Human Services. NAIC distributes publications on all aspects of adoption, including infant and international adoption, the adoption of children with special needs, and pertinent state and federal laws. For research, it provides a computerized information database containing titles and abstracts of books, articles, and program reports on adoption.

National Association of Black Social Workers (NABSW)
1220 11th St. NW, Suite 2, Washington, DC 20001
(202) 589-1850 • fax: (202) 589-1853
e-mail: ssw@unc.edu • Web site: http://ssw.unc.edu/professional/NABSW.html

NABSW seeks to support, develop, and sponsor programs and projects serving the interests of black communities. It is committed to a policy of same-race adoptions, promoting adoption of black children by black adoptive parents. NABSW publishes the annual *Black Caucus*.

National Coalition for Child Protection Reform (NCCPR)
53 Skyhill Rd., Suite 202, Alexandria, VA 22314
(703) 212-2006
e-mail: info@NCCPR.org • Web site: www.nccpr.org

NCCPR is a group of professionals who work to make the child welfare system better serve America's most vulnerable children by trying to change policies concerning child abuse, foster care, and family preservation. NCCPR advocates for systemic reform. The coalition does not provide advice in dealing with individual cases. It publishes issue papers on family preservation and foster care.

National Council for Adoption (NCFA)
225 N. Washington St., Alexandria, VA 22314-2561
(703) 299-6633 • fax: (703) 299-6004
e-mail: ncfa@adoptioncouncil.org • Web site: www.ncfa-usa.org

Representing volunteer agencies, adoptive parents, adoptees, and birth parents, NCFA works to protect the institution of adoption and to ensure the confidentiality of all involved in the adoption process. It strives for adoption regulations that will maintain the protection of birth parents, children, and adoptive parents. Its biweekly newsletter *Memo* provides updates on state and federal legislative and regulatory changes affecting adoption.

National Council for Single Adoptive Parents (NCSAP)
PO Box 55, Wharton, NJ 07885
(202) 966-6367
e-mail: ncsap@hotmail.com • Web site: www.adopting.org/ncsap.html

Formerly the Committee for Single Adoptive Parents (CSAP), the NCSAP is an information clearinghouse for singles who have adopted or who wish to adopt a child. It supports the adoption "of adoptable children to loving families, regardless of any difference in race, creed, color, religion or national origin, or of any handicap the children may have." CSAP refers interested individuals to local parent support groups and provides names of agencies that work with single adoptive parents. It publishes the *Handbook for Single Adoptive Parents* and a directory.

National Organization for Birthfathers and Adoption Reform (NOBAR)
PO Box 50, Punta Gorda, FL 33951-0050
(813) 637-7477

NOBAR is an advocacy group for men affected by adoption (including birth fathers of adoptees, divorced fathers whose children are or may be adopted by stepfathers, single fathers, and adoptive fathers). The organization promotes social policies and laws that protect the individual rights of those involved; it also works for the unrestricted opening of adoption records for birth parents and adoptees. NOBAR publishes *Birthfathers' Advocate*, a monthly newsletter.

North American Council on Adoptable Children (NACAC)
970 Raymond Ave., Suite 106, St. Paul, MN 55114-1149
(651) 644-3036 • fax: (651) 644-9848
e-mail: info@nacac.org • Web site: www.nacac.org

NACAC, an adoption advocacy organization, emphasizes special needs adoption, keeps track of adoption activities in each state, and promotes reform in adoption policies. NACAC publishes *Adoptalk* quarterly.

RainbowKids

1821 Commercial Dr., Suite S, Harvey, LA 70058
e-mail: letters@rainbowkids.com • Web site: www.rainbowkids.com

RainbowKids, the oldest and largest international adoption publication, helps families of internationally adopted children learn about international adoption, offers support during the adoption process, and provides resources to assist a newly adopted child adjust to his or her new family. The Web site has an archive of past articles written about subjects ranging from regular international adoption to adoption of special needs and older children.

Resolve, Inc.

7910 Woodmont Ave., Suite 1350, Bethesda, MD 20814
(301) 652-8585 • fax: (301) 652-9375
e-mail: resolveinc@aol.com • Web site: www.resolve.org

Resolve, Inc. is a nationwide information network serving the needs of men and women dealing with infertility and adoption issues. It publishes fact sheets and a quarterly national newsletter containing articles, medical information, and book reviews.

Reunite, Inc.

PO Box 694, Reynoldsburg, OH 43068

Reunite, Inc. promotes adoption reform, encourages legislative changes, and assists in searches for birth parents and adopted children. It publishes a brochure entitled *Reunite*.

BIBLIOGRAPHY

Books

Marie Adams	*Our Son, a Stranger: Adoption Breakdown and Its Effects on Parents.* Montreal: McGill-Queen's University Press, 2002.
David Brodzinsky et al.	*Being Adopted: The Lifelong Search for Self.* New York: Doubleday, 1992.
E. Wayne Carp, ed.	*Adoption in America: Historical Perspectives.* Ann Arbor: University of Michigan Press, 2002.
E. Wayne Carp, ed.	*Adoption Politics: Bastard Nation and Ballot Initiative 58.* Lawrence: University Press of Kansas, 2004.
Hawley Fogg-Davis	*The Ethics of Transracial Adoption.* Ithaca, NY: Cornell University Press, 2002.
James P. Gleeson and Creasie Finney Hairston, eds.	*Kinship Care: Improving Practice Through Research.* Washington, DC: CWLA, 1999.
Sally Haslanger and Charlotte Witt	*Adoption Matters: Philosophical and Feminist Essays.* Ithaca, NY: Cornell University Press, 2005.
Randall Kennedy	*Interracial Intimacies: Sex, Marriage, Identity, and Adoption.* New York: Pantheon, 2003.
Gail Kinn	*Be My Baby: Parents and Children Talk About Adoption.* New York: Artisan, 2000.
Betty Jean Lifton	*Journey of the Adopted Self: A Quest for Wholeness.* New York: BasicBooks, 1994.
Gerald P. Mallon	*Gay Men Choosing Parenthood.* New York: Columbia University Press, 2004.
Connaught Coyne Marshner, ed.	*Adoption Factbook III.* Washington, DC: National Council for Adoption, 1999.
Barbara Melosh	*Strangers and Kin: The American Way of Adoption.* Cambridge, MA: Harvard University Press, 2002.
Richard Mintzer	*Yes, You Can Adopt!* New York: Carroll & Graf, 2003.
Sandra Lee Patton	*BirthMarks: Transracial Adoption in Contemporary America.* New York: New York University Press, 2000.
Joyce Maguire Pavao	*The Family of Adoption.* Boston: Beacon, 1998.
Adam Pertman	*Adoption Nation: How the Adoption Revolution Is Transforming America.* New York: Basic Books, 2000.
Barbara Katz Rothman	*Weaving a Family: Untangling Race and Adoption.* Boston: Beacon, 2005.
Lita Linzer Schwartz and Florence W. Kaslow, eds.	*Welcome Home! An International and Nontraditional Adoption Reader.* Binghamton, NY: Haworth, 2003.

Liz Trinder et al.	*The Adoption Reunion Handbook*. Hoboken, NJ: John Wiley & Sons, 2004.
Nancy Newton Verrier	*The Primal Wound: Understanding the Adopted Child*. Baltimore: Gateway, 1993.
Katarina Wegar	*Adoption, Identity, and Kinship: The Debate over Sealed Birth Records*. New Haven, CT: Yale University Press, 1997.

Periodicals

L. Anne Babb	"Do Parents Matter?" *Adoptive Families*, January/February 1999.
Scott Baldauf	"Adoption with an Open Door for Birth Parents," *Christian Science Monitor*, October 21, 1998.
Nell Bernstein	"What Would YOU Have Done?" *Health*, March 2001.
Paula Bernstein	"Why I Don't Want to Find My Birth Mother," *Redbook*, March 2000.
Lisa Bohlander and Betsie Norris	"The Words We Use and the Messages They Convey," *Adoptive Families*, March/April 1998.
Kate Burke	"The Case for Open Adoption Records, a Decree," *American Adoption Congress*, Spring 1996.
Sarah Corbett	"Where Do Babies Come From?" *New York Times Magazine*, June 16, 2002.
Judith C. Daniluk and Joss Hurtig-Mitchell	"Themes of Hope and Healing: Infertile Couples' Experiences of Adoption," *Journal of Counseling & Development*, Fall 2003.
Sue Ferguson	"Leaving the Doors Open," *Maclean's*, July 26, 2004.
Robert L. Fischer	"The Emerging Role of Adoption Reunion Registries: Adoptee and Birthparent Views," *Child Welfare*, May/June 2002.
Susan Freinkel	"Who She Was," *Health*, July/August 2000.
Cynthia Hanson	"The Baby of Their Dreams," *Ladies' Home Journal*, April 2005.
Alexandra N. Helper	"The 'Motherless' Child: Some Issues in Adoption," *Psychiatric Times*, February 2005.
Leslie Doty Hollingsworth	"When an Adoption Disrupts: A Study of Public Attitudes," *Family Relations*, April 2003.
Pete Hudson and Karen Levasseur	"Supporting Foster Parents: Caring Voices," *Child Welfare*, November 2002.
Suein L. Hwang	"U.S. Adoptions Get Easier," *Wall Street Journal*, September 28, 2004.
Peter Jaret	"Saving Genia," *Health*, September 2004.
Richard Jerome and Joanne Fowler	"Second Time Around," *People*, September 3, 2001.

Tamar Lewin   "Two Views of Growing Up When the Faces Don't
                       Match," *New York Times*, October 27, 1998.

Laurie C. Miller   "International Adoption, Behavior, and Mental
                       Health," *Journal of the American Medical Association*,
                       May 25, 2005.

Christine Patrick   "International Adoptions: Myths and Realities,"
Mason Narad   *Pediatric Nursing*, November/December 2004.

Melba Newsome   "From Russia, with Love," *Parents*, September, 2004.

Marvin Olasky   "Forgotten Choice," *National Review*, March 10, 1997.

Jackie O'Neal   "White Parents Struggle to Adjust with Transracial
                       Adoptions," *New York Amsterdam News*, December 16,
                       2004.

Anne-Marie O'Neill   "Why Are American Babies Being Adopted Abroad?"
et al.   *People*, June 6, 2005.

Kit R. Roane   "Pitfalls for Parents," *U.S. News & World Report*, June 6,
                       2005.

Dan Savage   "Role Reversal," *New York Times Magazine*, March 11,
                       2001.

Brett S. Silverman   "The Winds of Change in Adoption Laws: Should
                       Adoptees Have Access to Adoption Records?" *Family
                       Court Review*, January 2001.

Rosemary Zibart   "Teens Wanted," *Time*, April 4, 2005.

Internet Sources

Randall Kennedy   "Interethnic Adoptions," FDCH congressional
                       testimony, September 15, 1998. http://waysandmeans.
                       house.gov/legacy/humres/105cong/9-15-98/9-15kenn.
                       htm.

National Adoption   "Access to Family Information by Adopted Persons."
Information   http://naic.acf.hhs.gov/general/legal/statues/info
Clearinghouse   accessap.pdf.

National Adoption   "Single Parent Adoption." http://naic.acf.hhs.gov/
Information   pubs/f_single/f_single.pdf.
Clearinghouse

INDEX